John Greenleaf Whittier

The Whittier year book

Passages from the verse and prose of John Greenleaf Whittier chosen for the daily

food

John Greenleaf Whittier

The Whittier year book

Passages from the verse and prose of John Greenleaf Whittier chosen for the daily food

ISBN/EAN: 9783337201272

Printed in Europe, USA, Canada, Australia, Japan

Cover: Foto ©Andreas Hilbeck / pixelio.de

More available books at **www.hansebooks.com**

THE WHITTIER YEAR BOOK
PASSAGES FROM THE VERSE AND PROSE
OF JOHN GREENLEAF WHITTIER
CHOSEN FOR THE DAILY
FOOD OF THE LOVER
OF THOUGHT AND
BEAUTY

BOSTON AND NEW YORK
HOUGHTON, MIFFLIN AND COMPANY
The Riverside Press, Cambridge

Copyright, 1895,
By HOUGHTON, MIFFLIN & CO.

All rights reserved.

The Riverside Press, Cambridge, Mass., U. S. A.
Electrotyped and Printed by H. O. Houghton & Co.

January

THE PAGEANT

A SOUND as if from bells of silver,
 Or elfin cymbals smitten clear,
 Through the frost-pictured panes I hear.

A brightness which outshines the morning,
 A splendor brooking no delay,
 Beckons and tempts my feet away.

I leave the trodden village highway
 For virgin snow-paths glimmering through
 A jewelled elm-tree avenue;

I tread in Orient halls enchanted,
 I dream the Saga's dream of caves
 Gem-lit beneath the North Sea waves!

I walk the land of Eldorado,
 I touch its mimic garden bowers,
 Its silver leaves and diamond flowers!

What miracle of weird transforming
 In this wild work of frost and light,
 This glimpse of glory infinite!

This foregleam of the Holy City,
 Like that to him of Patmos given,
 The white bride coming down from heaven!

JANUARY

1

Emancipation proclamation, 1863; Maria Edgeworth, 1767;
Arthur Hugh Clough, 1819.

NOT unto us who did but seek
The word that burned within to speak,
Not unto us this day belong
The triumph and exultant song.

Upon us fell in early youth
The burden of unwelcome truth,
And left us, weak and frail and few,
The censor's painful work to do.

Thenceforth our life a fight became,
The air we breathed was hot with blame;
For not with gauged and softened tone
We made the bondman's cause our own.
   HYMN FOR THE CELEBRATION OF EMANCIPATION.

2

James Wolfe, 1726; Justin Winsor, 1831.

DREARILY blows the north-wind
  From the land of ice and snow;
The eyes that look are weary,
  And heavy the hands that row.
And with one foot on the water,
  And one upon the shore,
The Angel of Shadow gives warning
  That day shall be no more.
         THE RED RIVER VOYAGEUR.

JANUARY

3

Lucretia Mott, 1793.

ONLY in the gathered silence
Of a calm and waiting frame,
Light and wisdom as from Heaven
To the seeker came.

Not to ease and aimless quiet
Doth that inward answer tend,
But to works of love and duty
As our being's end, —

Not to idle dreams and trances,
Length of face, and solemn tone,
But to Faith, in daily striving
And performance shown.
To ——.

4

Jakob Ludwig Grimm, 1785.

STILL linger in our noon of time
And on our Saxon tongue
The echoes of the home-born hymns
The Aryan mothers sung.

And childhood had its litanies
In every age and clime;
The earliest cradles of the race
Were rocked to poet's rhyme.
CHILD-SONGS.

JANUARY

5

Stephen Decatur, 1779.

SHUT in from all the world without,
We sat the clean-winged hearth about,
Content to let the north-wind roar
In baffled rage at pane and door,
While the red logs before us beat
The frost-line back with tropic heat;
And ever, when a louder blast
Shook beam and rafter as it passed,
The merrier up its roaring draught
The great throat of the chimney laughed.

. . . .

What matter how the night behaved?
What matter how the north-wind raved?
Blow high, blow low, not all its snow
Could quench our hearth-fire's ruddy glow.
SNOW-BOUND.

6

Epiphany; Charles Sumner, 1811.

YET, weak and blinded though we be,
   Thou dost our service own;
We bring our varying gifts to Thee,
   And Thou rejectest none.

O Love! O Life! Our faith and sight
   Thy presence maketh one,

JANUARY

As through transfigured clouds of white
We trace the noon-day sun.

So, to our mortal eyes subdued,
Flesh-veiled, but not concealed,
We know in Thee the fatherhood
And heart of God revealed.
OUR MASTER.

ONE language held his heart and lip,
Straight onward to his goal he trod,
And proved the highest statesmanship
Obedience to the voice of God.
SUMNER.

7

Israel Putnam, 1718.

AT times I long for gentler skies,
And bathe in dreams of softer air,
But homesick tears would fill the eyes
That saw the Cross without the Bear.
The pine must whisper to the palm,
The north-wind break the tropic calm;
And with the dreamy languor of the Line,
The North's keen virtue blend, and strength to
beauty join.
THE LAST WALK IN AUTUMN.

8

Robert Schumann, 1810; L. Alma Tadema, 1836.

LIKE warp and woof all destinies
Are woven fast,

JANUARY

Linked in sympathy like the keys
Of an organ vast.

Pluck one thread, and the web ye mar;
Break but one
Of a thousand keys, and the paining jar
Through all will run.
MY SOUL AND I.

9
John K. Paine, 1839.

WE looked upon a world unknown,
On nothing we could call our own.
Around the glistening wonder bent
The blue walls of the firmament,
No cloud above, no earth below, —
A universe of sky and snow!
The old familiar sights of ours
Took marvellous shapes; strange domes and
    towers
Rose up where sty or corn-crib stood,
Or garden wall, or belt of wood;
A smooth white mound the brush-pile showed,
A fenceless drift what once was road;
The bridle-post an old man sat
With loose-flung coat and high cocked hat:
The well-curb had a Chinese roof;
And even the long sweep, high aloof,
In its slant splendor, seemed to tell
Of Pisa's leaning miracle.
SNOW-BOUND.

JANUARY

10

Ethan Allen, 1737; Aubrey de Vere, 1814.

THE threads our hands in blindness spin
No self-determined plan weaves in;
The shuttle of the unseen powers
Works out a pattern not as ours.

Ah! small the choice of him who sings
What sound shall leave the smitten strings;
Fate holds and guides the hand of art;
The singer's is the servant's part.
OVERRULED.

11

Alexander Hamilton, 1757; Bayard Taylor, 1825.

HE brought us wonders of the new and old;
  We shared all climes with him. The Arab's tent
  To him its story-telling secret lent.
And, pleased, we listened to the tales he told.
His task, beguiled with songs that shall endure,
  In manly, honest thoroughness he wrought;
  From humble home-lays to the heights of thought
Slowly he climbed, but every step was sure.
BAYARD TAYLOR.

12

John Winthrop, 1588; John Hancock, 1737.

STERNLY faithful to duty, in peril, and suffering, and self-denial, they wrought out the noblest of

JANUARY

historical epics on the rough soil of New England.
They lived a truer poetry than Homer or Virgil
wrote.
PAWTUCKET FALLS.

13

S. P. Chase, 1808.

THE joy that comes in sorrow's guise,
The sweet pains of self-sacrifice,
I would not have them otherwise.

I suffer with no vain pretence
Of triumph over flesh and sense,
Yet trust the grievous providence,

How dark soe'er it seems, may tend,
By ways I cannot comprehend,
To some unguessed benignant end;

That every loss and lapse may gain
The clear-aired heights by steps of pain,
And never cross is borne in vain.
MY TRUST.

14

WHAT matter though we seek with pain
The garden of the gods in vain,
If lured thereby we climb to greet
Some wayside blossom Eden-sweet?

JANUARY

To seek is better than to gain,
The fond hope dies as we attain;
Life's fairest things are those which seem,
The best is that of which we dream.
Seeking of the Waterfall.

15

Molière, 1622; Marjorie Fleming, 1803.

Nor sky, nor wave, nor tree, nor flower,
  Nor green earth's virgin sod,
So moved the singer's heart of old
  As these small ones of God.

The mystery of unfolding life
  Was more than dawning morn,
Than opening flower or crescent moon
  The human soul new-born!

And still to childhood's sweet appeal
  The heart of genius turns,
And more than all the sages teach
  From lisping voices learns.
Child-Songs.

16

Edmund Spenser, died 1599.

I love the old melodious lays
Which softly melt the ages through,
  The songs of Spenser's golden days,

JANUARY

Arcadian Sidney's silvery phrase,
Sprinkling our noon of time with freshest morning
  dew.

Yet vainly in my quiet hours
To breathe their marvellous notes I try;
  I feel them, as the leaves and flowers
  In silence feel the dewy showers,
And drink with glad, still lips the blessing of the
  sky.
PROEM.

17

Benjamin Franklin, 1706; George Fuller, 1822.

THE riches of the Commonwealth
Are free, strong minds, and hearts of health;
And more to her than gold or grain,
The cunning hand and cultured brain.
OUR STATE.

HAUNTED of Beauty, like the marvellous youth
Who sang Saint Agnes' Eve! How passing fair
Her shapes took color in thy homestead air!
How on thy canvas even her dreams were truth!
Magician! who from commonest elements
Called up divine ideals, clothed upon
By mystic lights soft blending into one
Womanly grace and child-like innocence.
Teacher! thy lesson was not given in vain.
Beauty is goodness; ugliness is sin:
Art's place is sacred: nothing foul therein
May crawl or tread with bestial feet profane.

JANUARY

If rightly choosing is the painter's test,
Thy choice, O master, ever was the best.
AN ARTIST OF THE BEAUTIFUL.

18

Montesquieu, 1689; Daniel Webster, 1782.

THOU,
Whom the rich heavens did so endow
With eyes of power and Jove's own brow,
With all the massive strength that fills
Thy home-horizon's granite hills,
New England's stateliest type of man,
In port and speech Olympian;
Whom no one met, at first, but took
A second awed and wondering look.
Whose words in simplest homespun clad,
The Saxon strength of Cædmon's had,
With power reserved at need to reach
The Roman forum's loftiest speech.
Sweet with persuasion, eloquent
In passion, cool in argument,
Or, ponderous, falling on thy foes
As fell the Norse god's hammer blows,
And failing only when they tried
The adamant of the righteous side.
THE LOST OCCASION.

19

James Watt, 1736; Bernardin St. Pierre, 1737.

ALL who, by skill and patience, anyhow
Make service noble, and the earth redeem

JANUARY

From savageness. By kingly accolade
Than theirs was never worthier knighthood made.
THE PROBLEM.

HIS simple tale of love and woe
All hearts had melted, high or low; —
A blissful pain, a sweet distress,
Immortal in its tenderness.
CHAPEL OF THE HERMITS.

20

N P. Willis, 1807.

HE comes, — he comes, — the Frost Spirit comes!
— from the frozen Labrador, —
From the icy bridge of the Northern seas, which the white bear wanders o'er, —
Where the fisherman's sail is stiff with ice, and the luckless forms below
In the sunless cold of the lingering night into marble statues grow!

He comes, — he comes, — the Frost Spirit comes! and the quiet lake shall feel
The torpid touch of his glazing breath, and ring to the skater's heel;
And the streams which danced on the broken rocks, or sang to the leaning grass,
Shall bow again to their winter chain, and in mournful silence pass.
THE FROST SPIRIT.

JANUARY

21

Oscar II. of Sweden, 1829.

THE pause before the breaking seals
  Of mystery is this;
Yon miracle-play of night and day
  Makes dumb its witnesses.
What unseen altar crowns the hills
  That reach up stair on stair?
What eyes look through, what white wings fan
  These purple veils of air?
What Presence from the heavenly heights
  To those of earth stoops down?
Not vainly Hellas dreamed of gods
  On Ida's snowy crown!
                    SUNSET ON THE BEARCAMP.

22

Bacon, 1561; Lessing, 1729; Byron, 1788.

WHAT lack of goodly company,
  When masters of the ancient lyre
Obey my call, and trace for me
  Their words of mingled tears and fire!
I talk with Bacon, grave and wise,
I read the world with Pascal's eyes;
And priest and sage, with solemn brows austere,
And poets, garland-bound, the Lords of Thought,
    draw near.
                    THE LAST WALK IN AUTUMN.

13

JANUARY

23
William Page, 1811.

WISELY and well said the Eastern bard:
Fear is easy, but love is hard;
Easy to glow with the Santon's rage,
And walk on the Meccan pilgrimage;
But he is greatest and best who can
Worship Allah by loving man.
THE PREACHER.

24
Frederick the Great, 1712; Charles James Fox, 1749.

Is there, then, no death for a word once spoken?
Was never a deed but left its token
Written on tables never broken?

Do the elements subtle reflections give?
Do pictures of all the ages live
On Nature's infinite negative?
THE PALATINE.

25
Robert Burns, 1759.

I MATCHED with Scotland's heathery hills
    The sweetbrier and the clover;
With Ayr and Doon, my native rills,
    Their wood hymns chanting over.

JANUARY

O'er rank and pomp, as he had seen,
   I saw the Man uprising;
No longer common or unclean,
   The child of God's baptizing!

With clearer eyes I saw the worth
   Of life among the lowly;
The Bible at his Cotter's hearth
   Had made my own more holy.
                                            BURNS.

26

B. R. Haydon, 1786; Thomas Noon Talfourd, 1795.

YET do thy work; it shall succeed
   In thine or in another's day;
And, if denied the victor's meed,
   Thou shalt not lack the toiler's pay.

Faith shares the future's promise; Love's
   Self-offering is a triumph won;
And each good thought or action moves
   The dark world nearer to the sun.
                                         THE VOICES.

27

Mozart, 1756; Emperor William II., 1859.

FOLLY and Fear are sisters twain:
   One closing her eyes,
The other peopling the dark inane
   With spectral lies.

JANUARY

Know well, my soul, God's hand controls
    Whate'er thou fearest;
Round Him in calmest music rolls
    Whate'er thou hearest.

What to thee is shadow, to Him is day,
    And the end He knoweth,
And not on a blind and aimless way
    The spirit goeth.

                    MY SOUL AND I.

28

Charles George Gordon, 1833.

O HEART of mine, keep patience!— Looking forth,
    As from the Mount of Vision, I behold,
Pure, just, and free, the Church of Christ on earth,—
    The martyr's dream, the golden age foretold!
And found, at last, the mystic Grail I see,
    Brimmed with His blessing, pass from lip to lip
In sacred pledge of human fellowship;
And over all the songs of angels hear,—
Songs of the love that casteth out all fear,—
Songs of the Gospel of Humanity!

                    ON A PRAYER-BOOK.

29

Emanuel Swedenborg, 1688.

A MAN remarkable for his practical activities, an ardent scholar of the exact sciences, versed in all

JANUARY

the arcana of physics, a skilful and inventive mechanician, he has evolved from the hard and gross materialism of his studies a system of transcendent spiritualism. From his aggregation of cold and apparently lifeless practical facts beautiful and wonderful abstractions start forth like blossoms on the rod of the Levite.
SWEDENBORG

30

Walter Savage Landor, 1775.

To be saved is only this, —
Salvation from our selfishness;
From more than elemental fire, —
The soul's unsanctified desire;—
From sin itself, and not the pain
That warns us of its chafing chain.
THE MEETING.

31

Franz Schubert, 1797.

BETTER to stem with heart and hand
The roaring tide of life, than lie,
Unmindful, on its flowery strand,
Of God's occasions drifting by!
Better with naked nerve to bear
The needles of this goading air,
Than, in the lap of sensual ease, forego
The godlike power to do, the godlike aim to know.
THE LAST WALK IN AUTUMN.

February

THE CLEAR VISION.

I DID but dream. I never knew
    What charms our sternest season wore.
Was never yet the sky so blue,
    Was never earth so white before.
Till now I never saw the glow
Of sunset on yon hills of snow,
And never learned the bough's designs
Of beauty in its leafless lines.

Did ever such a morning break
    As that my eastern windows see?
Did ever such a moonlight take
    Weird photographs of shrub and tree?
Rang ever bells so wild and fleet
The music of the winter street?
Was ever yet a sound by half
So merry as yon school-boy's laugh?

O Earth! with gladness overfraught,
    No added charm thy face hath found;
Within my heart the change is wrought,
    My footsteps make enchanted ground.
From couch of pain and curtained room
Forth to thy light and air I come,
To find in all that meets my eyes
The freshness of a glad surprise.

FEBRUARY

Break forth, my lips, in praise, and own
  The wiser love severely kind;
Since, richer for its chastening grown,
  I see, whereas I once was blind.
The world, O Father! hath not wronged
With loss the life by Thee prolonged;
But still, with every added year,
More beautiful Thy works appear!

As Thou hast made thy world without,
  Make Thou more fair my world within;
Shine through its lingering clouds of doubt;
  Rebuke its haunting shapes of sin;
Fill, brief or long, my granted span
Of life with love to thee and man;
Strike when thou wilt the hour of rest,
But let my last days be my best!

FEBRUARY

1

Edmund Quincy, 1808.

BETTER than self-indulgent years
The outflung heart of youth,
Than pleasant songs in idle years
The tumult of the truth.

Rest for the weary hands is good,
And love for hearts that pine,
But let the manly habitude
Of upright souls be mine.

My Birthday.

2

Candlemas; Hannah More 1745.

WHATEVER in love's name is truly done
To free the bound and lift the fallen one
Is done to Christ. Whoso in deed and word
Is not against Him labors for our Lord.
When He, who, sad and weary, longing sore
For love's sweet service, sought the sisters' door,
One saw the heavenly, one the human guest,
But who shall say which loved the Master best?

By Their Works.

3

Mendelssohn, 1809; F. W. Robertson, 1816; Sidney Lanier, 1842.

A LIFE of beauty lends to all it sees
The beauty of its thought;

FEBRUARY

And fairest forms and sweetest harmonies
Make glad its way, unsought.

Sure stands the promise, — ever to the meek
A heritage is given;
Nor lose they Earth who, single-hearted, seek
The righteousness of Heaven!
THE CHRISTIAN TOURISTS.

4

Josiah Quincy, 1772.

THE moon above the eastern wood
Shone at its full; the hill-range stood
Transfigured in the silver flood,
Its blown snows flashing cold and keen,
Dead white, save where some sharp ravine
Took shadow, or the sombre green
Of hemlocks turned to pitchy black
Against the whiteness at their back.
For such a world and such a night
Most fitting that unwarming light,
Which only seemed where'er it fell
To make the coldness visible.
SNOW-BOUND.

5

James Otis, 1725; Sir Robert Peel, 1788.

OUR fathers to their graves have gone;
Their strife is past, — their triumph won;

FEBRUARY

But sterner trials wait the race
Which rises in their honored place, —
A moral warfare with the crime
And folly of an evil time.
                THE MORAL WARFARE.

6

Madame de Sévigné, 1626; Queen Anne, 1665.

WE shape ourselves the joy or fear
  Of which the coming life is made,
And fill our Future's atmosphere
  With sunshine or with shade.

The tissue of the Life to be
  We weave with colors all our own,
And in the field of Destiny
  We reap as we have sown.

Still shall the soul around it call
  The shadows which it gathered here,
And, painted on the eternal wall,
  The Past shall reappear.
                RAPHAEL.

7

Charles Dickens, 1812.

SOMETIMES glimpses on my sight,
Through present wrong, the eternal right;
And, step by step, since time began,
I see the steady gain of man;

FEBRUARY

That all of good the past hath had
Remains to make our own time glad,
Our common daily life divine,
And every land a Palestine.
THE CHAPEL OF THE HERMITS.

8

Robert Burton, 1577; John Ruskin, 1819.

THE airs of heaven blow o'er me;
A glory shines before me
Of what mankind shall be, —
Pure, generous, brave, and free.

A dream of man and woman
Diviner but still human,
Solving the riddle old,
Shaping the Age of Gold!

The love of God and neighbor;
An equal-handed labor;
The richer life, where beauty
Walks hand in hand with duty.
MY TRIUMPH.

9

James Parton, 1822.

WE dwell with fears on either hand,
  Within a daily strife,

FEBRUARY

And spectral problems waiting stand
Before the gates of life.

The doubts we vainly seek to solve,
  The truths we know, are one;
The known and nameless stars revolve
  Around the Central Sun.

And if we reap as we have sown,
  And take the dole we deal,
The law of pain is love alone,
  The wounding is to heal.
THE OLD BURYING-GROUND.

10

Charles Lamb, 1775; Ary Scheffer, 1795.

Lo! in the midst, with the same look he wore,
Healing and blessing on Gennesaret's shore,
Folding together, with the all-tender might
Of his great love, the dark hands and the white,
  Stands the Consoler, soothing every pain,
Making all burdens light, and breaking every chain.
ON A PRAYER-BOOK.

11

Lydia Maria Child, 1802; T. A. Edison, 1847.

AND, hushed to silence by a reverent awe,
  Methought, O friend, I saw
In thy true life of word and work and thought
  The proof of all we sought.

FEBRUARY

Did we not witness in the life of thee
    Immortal prophecy?
And feel, when with thee, that thy footsteps trod
    An everlasting road?

Not for brief days thy generous sympathies,
    Thy scorn of selfish ease;
Not for the poor prize of an earthly goal
    Thy strong uplift of soul.
WITHIN THE GATE.

12

Cotton Mather, 1663; Abraham Lincoln, 1809; Charles Robert Darwin, 1809; W. W. Story, 1819; George Meredith, 1828.

THAT quaint *Magnalia Christi*, with all strange and marvellous things,
Heaped up huge and undigested, like the chaos Ovid sings.
THE GARRISON OF CAPE ANN.

THE cloudy sign, the fiery guide,
    Along his pathway ran,
And Nature, through his voice, denied
    The ownership of man.

We rest in peace where these sad eyes
    Saw peril, strife, and pain;
His was the nation's sacrifice,
    And ours the priceless gain.
THE EMANCIPATION GROUP.

FEBRUARY

13

John Hunter, 1728.

DOUBTS to the world's child-heart unknown
Question us now from star and stone;
Too little or too much we know,
And sight is swift and faith is slow;
The power is lost to self-deceive
With shallow forms of make-believe.
We walk at high noon, and the bells
Call to a thousand oracles.
THE MEETING.

14

Edmond About, 1828.

WE share our primal parents' fate,
   And, in our turn and day,
Look back on Eden's sworded gate
   As sad and lost as they.

But still for us his native skies
   The pitying Angel leaves,
And leads through Toil to Paradise
   New Adams and new Eves!
A LAY OF OLD TIME.

15

S. Weir Mitchell, 1829.

NOT mine to look where cherubim
And seraphs may not see,

FEBRUARY

But nothing can be good in Him
    Which evil is in me.

The wrong that pains my soul below
    I dare not throne above,
I know not of His hate, — I know
    His goodness and His love.
                    THE ETERNAL GOODNESS.

16

Philip Melanchthon, 1497; Gaspard de Coligni, 1517.

IMMORTAL Love, forever full,
    Forever flowing free,
Forever shared, forever whole,
    A never-ebbing sea!

Our outward lips confess the name
    All other names above;
Love only knoweth whence it came
    And comprehendeth love.

Blow, winds of God, awake and blow
    The mists of earth away!
Shine out, O Light Divine, and show
    How wide and far we stray!
                      OUR MASTER.

17

A MIND rejoicing in the light
    Which melted through its graceful bower,

FEBRUARY

Leaf after leaf, dew-moist and bright,
And stainless in its holy white,
 Unfolding like a morning flower:
A heart, which, like a fine-toned lute,
 With every breath of feeling woke,
And, even when the tongue was mute,
 From eye and lip in music spoke.
MEMORIES.

18

Galileo, 1564; George Peabody, 1795.

No gain is lost; the clear-eyed saints look down
 Untroubled on the wreck of schemes and creeds;
 Love yet remains, its rosary of good deeds
Counting in task-field and o'erpeopled town.
Truth has charmed life; the Inward Word survives,
 And, day by day, its revelation brings;
 Faith, hope, and charity, whatsoever things
Which cannot be shaken, stand. Still holy lives
 Reveal the Christ of whom the letter told,
 And the new gospel verifies the old.
ADJUSTMENT.

19

Copernicus, 1473.

As night drew on, and, from the crest
Of wooded knolls that ridged the west,
The sun, a snow-blown traveller, sank
From sight beneath the smothering bank,

FEBRUARY

We piled, with care, our nightly stack
Of wood against the chimney-back, —
The oaken log, green, huge, and thick,
And on its top the stout back-stick;
The knotty forestick laid apart,
And filled between with curious art
The ragged brush; then, hovering near,
We watched the first red blaze appear,
Heard the sharp crackle, caught the gleam
On whitewashed wall and sagging beam,
Until the old, rude-furnished room
Burst, flower-like, into rosy bloom.
SNOW-BOUND.

20

David Garrick, 1716; Joseph Jefferson, 1829.

WHEN snow-flakes o'er the frozen earth,
   Instead of birds, are flitting,
When children throng the glowing hearth,
   And quiet wives are knitting;
While in the firelight strong and clear
   Young eyes of pleasure glisten,
To tales of all we see and hear
   The ears of home shall listen.
THE DROVERS.

21

John Henry Newman, 1801.

BY inward sense, by outward signs,
God's presence still the heart divines;

FEBRUARY

Through deepest joy of Him we learn,
In sorest grief to Him we turn,
And reason stoops its pride to share
The child-like instinct of a prayer.
MIRIAM.

22

Washington, 1732; James Russell Lowell, 1819.

THANK God! the people's choice was just,
The one man equal to his trust,
Wise beyond lore, and without weakness good,
Calm in the strength of flawless rectitude!
THE VOW OF WASHINGTON.

FROM purest wells of English undefiled
None deeper drank than he, the New World's child,
Who in the language of their farm-fields spoke
The wit and wisdom of New England folk,
Shaming a monstrous wrong. The world-wide
    laugh
Provoked thereby might well have shaken half
The walls of Slavery down, ere yet the ball
And mine of battle overthrew them all.
JAMES RUSSELL LOWELL.

23

G. F. Händel, 1685; Josiah Quincy, Jr., 1744.

HAST thou not, on some week of storm,
  Seen the sweet Sabbath breaking fair,
And cloud and shadow, sunlit, form
  The curtains of its tent of prayer?

FEBRUARY

So, haply, when thy task shall end,
The wrong shall lose itself in right,
And all thy week-day darkness blend
With the long Sabbath of the light!
THE VOICES.

24

George William Curtis, 1824.

THE jewels loosen on the branches,
And lightly, as the soft winds blow,
Fall, tinkling, on the ice below.

And through the clashing of their cymbals
I hear the old familiar fall
Of water down the rocky wall,

Where, from its wintry prison breaking,
In dark and silence hidden long,
The brook repeats its summer song;

One instant flashing in the sunshine,
Keen as a sabre from its sheath,
Then lost again the ice beneath.
THE PAGEANT.

25

AND if her life small leisure found
For feasting ear and eye,
And Pleasure, on her daily round,
She passed unpausing by,

FEBRUARY

Yet with her went a secret sense
 Of all things sweet and fair,
And Beauty's gracious providence
 Refreshed her unaware.

An inborn charm of graciousness
 Made sweet her smile and tone,
And glorified her farm-wife dress
 With beauty not its own.
            THE FRIEND'S BURIAL.

26

Arago, 1786; Victor Hugo, 1802.

THE mystery dimly understood,
That love of God is love of good,
That Book and Church and Day are given
For man, not God, — for earth, not heaven, —
The blessed means to holiest ends,
Not masters, but benignant friends.
            THE MEETING.

27

H. W. Longfellow, 1807; J. E. Renan, 1823.

THY greeting smile was pledge and prelude
 Of generous deeds and kindly words;
In thy large heart were fair guest-chambers,
 Open to sunrise and the birds!
            A MEMORIAL.

FEBRUARY

28

Montaigne, 1533.

SLOW passed that vision from my view,
  But not the lesson which it taught;
The soft, calm shadows which it threw
  Still rested on my thought:

The truth, that painter, bard, and sage,
  Even in Earth's cold and changeful clime,
Plant for their deathless heritage
  The fruits and flowers of time.

RAPHAEL.

29

Rossini, 1792.

BLAND as the morning breath of June
  The southwest breezes play;
And, through its haze, the winter noon
  Seems warm as summer's day.
The snow-plumed Angel of the North
  Has dropped his icy spear;
Again the mossy earth looks forth,
  Again the streams gush clear.

A DREAM OF SUMMER.

March

THE WIND OF MARCH.

Up from the sea the wild north wind is blowing
    Under the sky's gray arch;
Smiling, I watch the shaken elm-boughs, knowing
    It is the wind of March.

Between the passing and the coming season,
    This stormy interlude
Gives to our winter-wearied hearts a reason
    For trustful gratitude.

Welcome to waiting ears its harsh forewarning
    Of light and warmth to come.
The longed-for joy of Nature's Easter morning,
    The earth arisen in bloom!

In the loud tumult winter's strength is breaking;
    I listen to the sound,
As to a voice of resurrection, waking
    To life the dead, cold ground.

Between these gusts, to the soft lapse I hearken
    Of rivulets on their way;
I see these tossed and naked treetops darken
    With the fresh leaves of May.

MARCH

This roar of storm, this sky so gray and lowering,
    Invite the airs of Spring,
A warmer sunshine over fields of flowering,
    The bluebird's song and wing.

Closely behind, the Gulf's warm breezes follow
    This northern hurricane,
And, borne thereon, the bobolink and swallow
    Shall visit us again.

And, in green wood-paths, in the kine-fed pasture,
    And by the whispering rills,
Shall flowers repeat the lesson of the Master
    Taught on his Syrian hills.

Blow, then, wild wind! thy roar shall end in singing,
    Thy chill in blossoming;
Come, like Bethesda's troubling angel, bringing
    The healing of the Spring.

MARCH

1

Frédéric Chopin, 1809; W. D. Howells, 1837.

THE Night is mother of the Day,
  The Winter of the Spring,
And ever upon old Decay
  The greenest mosses cling.
Behind the cloud the starlight lurks,
  Through showers the sunbeams fall;
For God, who loveth all His works,
  Has left His hope with all!
                    A DREAM OF SUMMER.

2

Sir Thomas Bodley, 1544.

NEVER on custom's oilèd grooves
The world to a higher level moves,
But grates and grinds with friction hard
On granite boulder and flinty shard.
The heart must bleed before it feels,
The pool be troubled before it heals.
                    THE PREACHER.

3

Edmund Waller, 1606; William Godwin, 1756.

HE prayeth best who leaves unguessed
The mystery of another's breast.

MARCH

Why cheeks grow pale, why eyes o'erflow,
Or heads are white, thou need'st not know.
Enough to note by many a sign
That every heart hath needs like thine.
Pray for us!
THE PRAYER-SEEKER.

4

T. S. King, died 1864.

THE great work laid upon his twoscore years
Is done, and well done. If we drop our tears,
Who loved him as few men were ever loved,
We mourn no blighted hope nor broken plan
With him whose life stands rounded and approved
In the full growth and stature of a man.
Mingle, O bells, along the Western slope,
With your deep toll a sound of faith and hope!
Wave cheerily still, O banner half-way down,
From thousand-masted bay and steepled town!
Let the strong organ with its loftiest swell
Lift the proud sorrow of the land, and tell
That the brave sower saw his ripened grain.
O East and West! O morn and sunset twain
No more forever! — has he lived in vain
Who, priest of Freedom, made ye one, and told
Your bridal service from his lips of gold?
THOMAS STARR KING.

MARCH

5

James Madison, 1751.

WITH smoking axle hot with speed, with steeds of
  fire and steam,
Wide-waked To-day leaves Yesterday behind him
  like a dream.
Still, from the hurrying train of Life, fly backward
  far and fast
The milestones of the fathers, the landmarks of the
  past.
MARY GARVIN.

6

*Michelangelo, 1475; Elizabeth Barrett Browning, 1806; George du
Maurier, 1834.*

I KNOW not how, in other lands,
  The changing seasons come and go;
  What splendors fall on Syrian sands,
  What purple lights on Alpine snow!
Nor how the pomp of sunrise waits
On Venice at her watery gates;
A dream alone to me is Arno's vale,
And the Alhambra's halls are but a traveller's tale.
THE LAST WALK IN AUTUMN.

7

Sir John Herschel, 1792; Sir Edwin Landseer, 1802.

ENOUGH for me to feel and know
That He in whom the cause and end,

MARCH

The past and future, meet and blend, —
Who, girt with his Immensities,
Our vast and star-hung system sees,
Small as the clustered Pleiades, —
Moves not alone the heavenly quires,
But waves the spring-time's grassy spires,
Guards not archangel feet alone,
But deigns to guide and keep my own;
Speaks not alone the words of fate
Which worlds destroy and worlds create,
But whispers in my spirit's ear,
In tones of love, or warning fear,
A language none beside may hear.
QUESTIONS OF LIFE.

8

Sir William Hamilton, 1788.

So welcome I from every source
The tokens of that primal Force,
Older than heaven itself, yet new
As the young heart it reaches to,
Beneath whose steady impulse rolls
The tidal wave of human souls;
Guide, comforter, and inward word,
The eternal spirit of the Lord!
MIRIAM.

9

Mirabeau, 1749; William Cobbett, 1762.

THE wild March rains had fallen fast and long
The snowy mountains of the North among,

MARCH

Making each vale a watercourse, — each hill
Bright with the cascade of some new-made rill.

Gnawed by the sunbeams, softened by the rain,
Heaved underneath by the swollen current's strain,
The ice-bridge yielded, and the Merrimack
Bore the huge ruin crashing down its track.
THE BRIDAL OF PENNACOOK.

10

F. von Schlegel, 1772; William Etty, 1787.

FALSEHOODS which we spurn to-day
  Were the truths of long ago;
Let the dead boughs fall away,
  Fresher shall the living grow.
CALEF IN BOSTON.

11

Charles Sumner, died 1874.

THE old traditions of his State,
  The memories of her great and good,
Took from his life a fresher date,
  And in himself embodied stood.

Safely his dearest friends may own
  The slight defects he never hid,
The surface-blemish in the stone
  Of the tall, stately pyramid.

MARCH

Suffice it that he never brought
　His conscience to the public mart;
But lived himself the truth he taught,
　White-souled, clean-handed, pure of heart.
SUMNER.

12

Richard Steele, 1672; Bishop Berkeley, 1684; Mary Howitt, 1799.

THREE shades at this moment seem walking her strand,
Each with head halo-crowned, and with palms in his hand, —
Wise Berkeley, grave Hopkins, and, smiling serene
On prelate and puritan, Channing is seen.

One holy name bearing, no longer they need
Credentials of party, and passwords of creed:
The new song they sing hath a threefold accord,
And they own one baptism, one faith, and one Lord!
THE QUAKER ALUMNI.

13

Joseph Priestley, 1733.

THE wind-harp chooses not the tone
That through its trembling threads is blown;
The patient organ cannot guess
What hand its passive keys shall press.

MARCH

Through wish, resolve, and act, our will
Is moved by undreamed forces still;
And no man measures in advance
His strength with untried circumstance.
OVERRULED.

14

Victor Emanuel, 1820; Humbert, 1844.

As yonder tower outstretches to the earth
The dark triangle of its shade alone
When the clear day is shining on its top,
So, darkness in the pathway of Man's life
Is but the shadow of God's providence,
By the great Sun of Wisdom cast thereon;
And what is dark below is light in Heaven.
TAULER.

15

John Endicott, died 1665; Andrew Jackson, 1767.

A GRAVE, strong man, who knew no peer
In the pilgrim land, where he ruled in fear
Of God, not man, and for good or ill
Held his trust with an iron will.
THE KING'S MISSIVE.

16

Caroline Herschel, 1750.

FOR ages on our river borders,
  These tassels in their tawny bloom,

MARCH

And willowy studs of downy silver,
Have prophesied of Spring to come.

For ages have the unbound waters
Smiled on them from their pebbly hem,
And the clear carol of the robin
And song of bluebird welcomed them.
THE FIRST FLOWERS.

17

Madame Roland, 1754.

I AM: how little more I know!
Whence came I? Whither do I go?
A centred self, which feels and is;
A cry between the silences;
A shadow-birth of clouds at strife
With sunshine on the hills of life;
A shaft from Nature's quiver cast
Into the Future from the Past;
Between the cradle and the shroud,
A meteor's flight from cloud to cloud.
QUESTIONS OF LIFE.

18

Francis Lieber, 1800.

HEED how thou livest. Do no act by day
Which from the night shall drive thy peace away.
In months of sun so live that months of rain
Shall still be happy. Evermore restrain

MARCH

Evil and cherish good, so shall there be
Another and a happier life for thee.
CONDUCT.

19

A. P. Peabody, 1811; David Livingstone, 1813.

No fable old, nor mythic lore,
   Nor dream of bards and seers,
No dead fact stranded on the shore
   Of the oblivious years;—

But warm, sweet, tender, even yet
   A present help is He;
And faith has still its Olivet,
   And love is Galilee.
OUR MASTER.

20

Henrik Ibsen, 1828; Charles William Eliot, 1834.

Fresh and green from the rotting roots
Of primal forests the young growth shoots; . . .
On the ladder of God, which upward leads,
The step of progress are human needs.
For his judgments still are a mighty deep,
And the eyes of his providence never sleep.
THE PREACHER.

MARCH

21

J. S. Bach, 1685; Jean Paul Richter, 1763.

THE sweet persuasion of His voice
Respects thy sanctity of will.
He giveth day: thou hast thy choice
To walk in darkness still;

As one who, turning from the light,
Watches his own gray shadow fall,
Doubting, upon his path of night,
If there be day at all!

No word of doom may shut thee out,
No wind of wrath may downward whirl,
No swords of fire keep watch about
The open gates of pearl.
THE ANSWER.

22

Van Dyck, 1599; Rosa Bonheur, 1822; Randolph Caldecott, 1846.

THE Traveller said: "If songs have creeds,
Their choice of them let singers make;
But Art no other sanction needs
Than beauty for its own fair sake.
It grinds not in the mill of use,
Nor asks for leave, nor begs excuse;
It makes the flexile laws it deigns to own,
And gives its atmosphere its color and its tone."
THE TENT ON THE BEACH.

MARCH

23

P. L. de Laplace, 1749.

ABOVE, below, in sky and sod,
  In leaf and spar, in star and man,
Well might the wise Athenian scan
  The geometric signs of God,
  The measured order of His plan.

And India's mystics sang aright
  Of the One Life pervading all,—
  One Being's tidal rise and fall
In soul and form, in sound and sight,—
  Eternal outflow and recall.
                    THE OVER-HEART.

24

Joel Barlow, 1755; William Morris, 1834.

STILL, in perpetual judgment,
  I hold assize within,
With sure reward of holiness,
  And dread rebuke of sin.

A light, a guide, a warning,
  A presence ever near,
Through the deep silence of the flesh
  I reach the inward ear.

My Gerizim and Ebal
  Are in each human soul,

MARCH

> The still, small voice of blessing,
> And Sinai's thunder-roll.
> THE VISION OF ECHARD.

25

Antonio Rosmini, 1797.

It is not ours to separate
The tangled skein of will and fate,
To show what metes and bounds should stand
Upon the soul's debatable land,
And between choice and Providence
Divide the circle of events;
  But He who knows our frame is just,
Merciful and compassionate,
And full of sweet assurances
And hope for all the language is,
  That He remembereth we are dust!
SNOW-BOUND.

26

Count Rumford, 1753; Nathaniel Bowditch, 1773.

Nor fear I aught that science brings
From searching through material things;
Content to let its glasses prove,
Not by the letter's oldness move,
The myriad worlds on worlds that course
The spaces of the universe;
Since everywhere the Spirit walks
The garden of the heart, and talks
With man, as under Eden's trees,
In all his varied languages.
MIRIAM.

MARCH

27

AH, well! — The world is discreet;
   There are plenty to pause and wait;
But here was a man who set his feet
   Sometimes in advance of fate, —

Plucked off the old bark when the inner
   Was slow to renew it,
And put to the Lord's work the sinner
   When saints failed to do it.

To G. L. S.

28

Samuel Sewall, 1652; Thomas Clarkson, 1760.

STATELY and slow, with thoughtful air,
His black cap hiding his whitened hair,
Walks the Judge of the great Assize,
Samuel Sewall the good and wise.
His face with lines of firmness wrought,
He wears the look of a man unbought,
Who swears to his hurt and changes not;
Yet touched and softened, nevertheless,
With the grace of Christian gentleness, . . .
True and tender and brave and just,
That man might honor and woman trust.

  .   .   .   .

   Green forever the memory be
Of the Judge of the old Theocracy,

MARCH

Whom even his errors glorified,
Like a far-seen, sunlit mountain-side
By the cloudy shadows which o'er it glide!
THE PROPHECY OF SAMUEL SEWALL.

29

OVER the roofs of the pioneers
Gathers the moss of a hundred years;
On man and his works has passed the change
Which needs must be in a century's range.
The land lies open and warm in the sun,
Anvils clamor and mill-wheels run, —
Flocks on the hillsides, herds on the plain,
The wilderness gladdened with fruit and grain!
But the living faith of the settlers old
A dead profession their children hold; . . .
And earth, which seemed to the fathers meant
But as a pilgrim's wayside tent, —
A nightly shelter to fold away
When the Lord should call at the break of day, —
Solid and steadfast seems to be,
And Time has forgotten Eternity!
THE PREACHER.

30

F. A. G. Tholuck, 1799; John Fiske, 1842.

NOTHING fails of its end. Out of sight sinks the stone
In the deep sea of time, but the circles sweep on,

MARCH

Till the low-rippled murmurs along the shores run,
And the dark and dead waters leap glad in the sun.
THE QUAKER ALUMNI.

31

Andrew Marvell, 1621 ; Joseph Haydn, 1732 ; Edward Fitzgerald, 1809.

YET here at least an earnest sense
Of human right and weal is shown ;
A hate of tyranny intense,
And hearty in its vehemence,
As if my brother's pain and sorrow were my own.

O Freedom ! if to me belong
Nor mighty Milton's gift divine,
Nor Marvell's wit and graceful song,
Still with a love as deep and strong
As theirs, I lay, like them, my best gifts on thy shrine !
PROEM.

April

"The spring comes slowly up this way."
CHRISTABEL.

'T is the noon of the springtime, yet never a bird
In the wind-shaken elm or the maple is heard;
For green meadow-grasses wide levels of snow,
And blowing of drifts where the crocus should blow;
Where wind-flower and violet, amber and white,
On south-sloping brooksides should smile in the light,
O'er the cold winter-beds of their late-waking roots
The frosty flake eddies, the ice-crystal shoots;
And, longing for light, under wind-driven heaps,
Round the boles of the pine-wood the ground-laurel creeps,
Unkissed of the sunshine, unbaptized of showers,
With buds scarcely swelled, which should burst into flowers!
We wait for thy coming, sweet wind of the south!
For the touch of thy light wings, the kiss of thy mouth;
For the yearly evangel thou bearest from God,
Resurrection and life to the graves of the sod!

APRIL

1

Sir Thomas Fowell Buxton, 1786 ; Bismarck, 1815.

THANKS, Mary! for this wild-wood token
  Of Freya's footsteps drawing near;
Almost, as in the rune of Asgard,
  The growing of the grass I hear.

It is as if the pine-trees called me
  From ceilèd room and silent books,
To see the dance of woodland shadows,
  And hear the song of April brooks!
                        THE FIRST FLOWERS.

2

H. C. Andersen, 1805.

O THOU, who in the garden's shade
  Didst wake Thy weary ones again,
Who slumbered at that fearful hour
  Forgetful of Thy pain,

Bend o'er us now, as over them,
  And set our sleep-bound spirits free ;
Nor leave us slumbering in the watch
  Our souls should keep with Thee !
                    THE CYPRESS-TREE OF CEYLON.

APRIL

3

George Herbert, 1593; Washington Irving, 1783.

WE faintly hear, we dimly see,
   In differing phrase we pray;
But, dim or clear, we own in Thee
   The Light, the Truth, the Way!

No pride of self Thy service hath,
   No place for me and mine;
Our human strength is weakness, death
   Our life, apart from Thine.

Apart from Thee all gain is loss,
   All labor vainly done;
The solemn shadow of Thy Cross
   Is better than the sun.
                              OUR MASTER.

4

Benjamin Peirce, 1809; James Freeman Clarke, 1810.

ALAS for him who never sees
The stars shine through his cypress-trees!
Who, hopeless, lays his dead away,
Nor looks to see the breaking day
Aross the mournful marbles play!
Who hath not learned, in hours of faith,
   The truth to flesh and sense unknown,
That Life is ever lord of Death,
   And Love can never lose its own!
                              SNOW-BOUND.

APRIL

5

F. R. Stockton, 1834; A. C. Swinburne, 1837.

O SOUL of the springtime, its light and its breath,
Bring warmth to this coldness, bring life to this death ;
Renew the great miracle ; let us behold
The stone from the mouth of the sepulchre rolled.
Let our faith, which in darkness and coldness has lain,
Revive with the warmth and the brightness again,
And in blooming of flower and budding of tree
The symbols and types of our destiny see.
APRIL.

6

Raphael, 1483, and died 1520.

AROUND the mighty master came
   The marvels which his pencil wrought,
Those miracles of power whose fame
   Is wide as human thought.

There drooped thy more than mortal face,
   O Mother, beautiful and mild !
Enfolding in one dear embrace
   Thy Saviour and thy Child !

The rapt brow of the Desert John ;
   The awful glory of that day
When all the Father's brightness shone
   Through manhood's veil of clay.
RAPHAEL.

APRIL

7

William Wordsworth, 1770; W. E. Channing, 1780.

THE violet by its mossy stone,
 The primrose by the river's brim,
And chance-sown daffodil, have found
 Immortal life through him.

The sunrise on his breezy lake,
 The rosy tints his sunset brought,
World-seen, are gladdening all the vales
 And mountain-peaks of thought.

Art builds on sand; the works of pride
 And human passion change and fall;
But that which shares the life of God
 With Him surviveth all.

WORDSWORTH.

8

David Rittenhouse, 1732.

A CHARMÈD life unknown to death,
Immortal freshness Nature hath;
 Her fabled fount and glen
Are now and here: Dodona's shrine
Still murmurs in the wind-swept pine, —
 All is that e'er hath been.

To ——.

APRIL

9

Fisher Ames, 1758.

I WANDERED lonely where the pine-trees made
Against the bitter East their barricade,
   And, guided by its sweet
Perfume, I found, within a narrow dell,
The trailing spring flower tinted like a shell
   Amid dry leaves and mosses at my feet.

From under dead boughs, for whose loss the pines
Moaned ceaseless overhead, the blossoming vines
   Lifted their glad surprise,
While yet the bluebird smoothed in leafless trees
His feathers ruffled by the chill sea-breeze,
   And snowdrifts lingered under April skies.
THE TRAILING ARBUTUS.

10

C. F. S. Hahnemann, 1755.

GOD pity them both! and pity us all,
Who vainly the dreams of youth recall.

For, of all sad words of tongue or pen,
The saddest are these: "It might have been!"

Ah, well! for us all some sweet hope lies
Deeply buried from human eyes;

And, in the hereafter, angels may
Roll the stone from its grave away!
MAUD MULLER.

APRIL

11

George Canning, 1770; Edward Everett, 1794.

WE have seen, in these years of trial, very great sacrifices offered upon the altar of patriotism, — wealth, ease, home-love, life itself. But Edward Everett did more than this: he laid on that altar not only his time, talents, and culture, but his pride of opinion, his long-cherished views of policy, his personal and political predilections, and his constitutional fastidiousness of conservatism. With a rare and noble magnanimity, he met, without hesitation, the demand of the great occasion. All honor to him!

EDWARD EVERETT.

12

Henry Clay, 1777.

MAN, who walketh in a show,
Sees before him, to and fro,
Shadow and illusion go;
All things flow and fluctuate,
Now contract and now dilate;
In the welter of this sea,
Nothing stable is but Thee!

ANDREW RYKMAN'S PRAYER.

APRIL

13

Madame Guyon, 1648.

NOT with hatred's undertow
Doth the Love Eternal flow;
Every chain that spirits wear
Crumbles in the breath of prayer;
And the penitent's desire
Opens every gate of fire.

Still Thy love, O Christ arisen,
Yearns to reach these souls in prison!
Through all depths of sin and loss
Drops the plummet of Thy cross!
Never yet abyss was found
Deeper than that cross could sound!
THE GRAVE BY THE LAKE.

14

Horace Bushnell, 1802.

AND all about the softening air
  Of new-born sweetness tells;
And the ungathered Mayflowers wear
  The tints of ocean shells.

The old, assuring miracle
  Is fresh as heretofore;
And earth takes up its parable
  Of life from death once more.
THE FRIEND'S BURIAL.

APRIL

15

L. A. Thiers, 1797; J. L. Motley, 1814; Henry James, 1843.

DEATH called him from a need as imminent
As that from which the Silent William went
When powers of evil, like the smiting seas
On Holland's dikes, assailed her liberties.
Sadly, while yet in doubtful balance hung
The weal and woe of France, the bells were rung
For her lost leader. Paralyzed of will,
Above his bier the hearts of men stood still.
Then, as if set to his dead lips, the horn
Of Roland wound once more to rouse and warn,
The old voice filled the air! His last brave word
Not vainly France to all her boundaries stirred.
Strong as in life, he still for Freedom wrought,
As the dead Cid at red Toloso fought.
                                    THIERS.

16

Sir John Franklin, 1786; William Chambers, 1800.

SAD it is the mournful yew-tree
    O'er his slumbers may not wave;
Sad it is the English daisy
    May not blossom on his grave.

But his tomb shall storm and winter
    Shape and fashion year by year,
Pile his mighty mausoleum,
    Block by block, and tier on tier.
                                LADY FRANKLIN.

APRIL

17

William Gilmore Simms, 1806.

LIGHT, warmth, and sprouting greenness, and o'er all
Blue, stainless, steel-bright ether, raining down
Tranquillity upon the deep-hushed town,
The freshening meadows, and the hillsides brown;
    Voice of the west-wind from the hills of pine,
And the brimmed river from its distant fall,
  Low hum of bees, and joyous interlude
  Of bird-songs in the streamlet-skirting wood, —
Heralds and prophecies of sound and sight, . . .
Once more, through God's great love, with you I share
A morn of resurrection sweet and fair
    As that which saw, of old, in Palestine,
  Immortal Love uprising in fresh bloom
  From the dark night and winter of the tomb!
                           PICTURES.

18

I MOURN no more my vanished years:
    Beneath a tender rain,
An April rain of smiles and tears,
    My heart is young again.

APRIL

The west-winds blow, and, singing low,
  I hear the glad streams run;
The windows of my soul I throw
  Wide open to the sun.
                                    MY PSALM.

19

Lexington and Concord, 1775.

THEY went where duty seemed to call,
  They scarcely asked the reason why;
  They only knew they could but die,
And death was not the worst of all!

Of man for man the sacrifice,
  All that was theirs to give, they gave.
  The flowers that blossomed from their grave
Have sown themselves beneath all skies.

Their death-shot shook the feudal tower,
  And shattered slavery's chain as well;
  On the sky's dome, as on a bell,
Its echo struck the world's great hour.
                                    LEXINGTON.

20

W. H. Furness, 1802.

No offering of my own I have,
  Nor works my faith to prove;

APRIL

I can but give the gifts He gave,
And plead His love for love.

And so beside the Silent Sea
I wait the muffled oar;
Nor harm from Him can come to me
On ocean or on shore.

I know not where His islands lift
Their fronded palms in air;
I only know I cannot drift
Beyond His love and care.
THE ETERNAL GOODNESS.

21

Reginald Heber, 1783; James Martineau, 1805; Charlotte Brontë, 1816; H. A. Taine, 1828.

GIVE human nature reverence for the sake
Of One who bore it, making it divine
With the ineffable tenderness of God!
Let common need, the brotherhood of prayer,
The heirship of an unknown destiny,
The unsolved mystery round about us, make
A man more precious than the Gold of Ophir!
AMONG THE HILLS.

22

Henry Fielding, 1707; Madame de Stael, 1766.

THE stream is brightest at its spring,
And blood is not like wine:

APRIL

Nor honored less than he who heirs
Is he who founds a line.

Full lightly shall the prize be won,
    If Love be Fortune's spur;
And never maiden stoops to him
    Who lifts himself to her.

Oh, rank is good, and gold is fair,
    And high and low mate ill;
But love has never known a law
    Beyond its own sweet will!
                  AMY WENTWORTH.

23

St. George; Shakespeare, 1564, and died 1616.

AND here, to-day, the dead look down,
The kings of mind again we crown;
We hear the voices lost so long,
The sage's word, the sibyl's song.

Here Greek and Roman find themselves
Alive along these crowded shelves;
And Shakespeare treads again his stage,
And Chaucer paints anew his age.

As if some Pantheon's marbles broke
Their stony trance, and lived and spoke,
Life thrills along the alcoved hall,
The lords of thought await our call!
                    THE LIBRARY.

APRIL

24

Anthony Trollope, 1815; J. T. Fields, died 1881.

KEEP for us, O friend, where'er
Thou art waiting, all that here
Made thy earthly presence dear;

Something of thy pleasant past
On a ground of wonder cast,
In the stiller waters glassed!

Keep the human heart of thee;
Let the mortal only be
Clothed in immortality.

And when fall our feet as fell
Thine upon the asphodel,
Let thy old smile greet us well;

Proving in a world of bliss
What we fondly dream in this, —
Love is one with holiness!
IN MEMORY.

25

Oliver Cromwell, 1599; John Keble, 1792.

NOT untrue that tale of old!
Now, as then, the wise and bold
All the powers of Nature hold
  Subject to their kingly will;

64

APRIL

> From the wondering crowds ashore,
> Treading life's wild waters o'er,
> As upon a marble floor,
>   Moves the strong man still.
> THE BRIDAL OF PENNACOOK.

26

David Hume, 1711; Uhland, 1787; Alice Cary, 1820.

> HER dark, dilating eyes expressed
> The broad horizons of the west;
> Her speech dropped prairie flowers; the gold
> Of harvest wheat about her rolled.
>
> . . . .
>
> Again the blackbirds sing; the streams
> Wake, laughing, from their winter dreams,
> And tremble in the April showers
> The tassels of the maple flowers.
>
> But not for her has spring renewed
> The sweet surprises of the wood;
> And bird and flower are lost to her
> Who was their best interpreter!
> THE SINGER.

27

S. F. B. Morse, 1791; Louis Kossuth, 1806; Herbert Spencer, 1820.

> TYPE of two mighty continents! — combining
>   The strength of Europe with the warmth and glow

APRIL

Of Asian song and prophecy, — the shining
Of Orient splendors over Northern snow!
To Kossuth.

From clime to clime, from shore to shore,
  Shall thrill the magic thread;
The new Prometheus steals once more
  The fire that wakes the dead.
The Cable Hymn.

28

Earl of Shaftesbury, 1801.

There are, who, like the Seer of old,
  Can see the helpers God has sent,
And how life's rugged mountain-side
  Is white with many an angel tent!

They hear the heralds whom our Lord
  Sends down his pathway to prepare;
And light, from others hidden, shines
  On their high place of faith and prayer.

Let such, for earth's despairing ones,
  Hopeless, yet longing to be free,
Breathe once again the Prophet's prayer:
  "Lord, ope their eyes, that they may see!"
The Legend of St. Mark.

APRIL

29

Oliver Ellsworth, 1745.

SOMEWHAT of goodness, something true
From sun and spirit shining through
All faiths, all worlds, as through the dark
Of ocean shines the lighthouse spark,
Attests the presence everywhere
Of love and providential care.
MIRIAM.

30

First Inauguration of Washington, 1789.

O CITY sitting by the Sea!
How proud the day that dawned on thee,
When the new era, long desired, began,
And, in its need, the hour had found the man!

How felt the land in every part
The strong throb of a nation's heart,
As its great leader gave, with reverent awe,
His pledge to Union, Liberty, and Law!

. . . .

Lo! where with patient toil he nursed
And trained the new-set plant at first,
The widening branches of a stately tree
Stretch from the sunrise to the sunset sea.

APRIL

One people now, all doubt beyond,
His name shall be our Union-bond;
We lift our hands to Heaven, and here and now
Take on our lips the old Centennial vow.
THE VOW OF WASHINGTON.

May

MY PLAYMATE

THE pines were dark on Ramoth hill,
  Their song was soft and low;
The blossoms in the sweet May wind
  Were falling like the snow.

The blossoms drifted at our feet,
  The orchard birds sang clear;
The sweetest and the saddest day
  It seemed of all the year.

For, more to me than birds or flowers,
  My playmate left her home,
And took with her the laughing spring,
  The music and the bloom.

She kissed the lips of kith and kin,
  She laid her hand in mine;
What more could ask the bashful boy
  Who fed her father's kine?

She left us in the bloom of May:
  The constant years told o'er
Their seasons with as sweet May morns,
  But she came back no more.

. . . .

MAY

The wild grapes wait us by the brook,
  The brown nuts on the hill,
And still the May-day flowers make sweet
  The woods of Follymill.

The lilies blossom in the pond,
  The bird builds in the tree,
The dark pines sing on Ramoth hill
  The slow song of the sea.

O playmate in the golden time!
  Our mossy seat is green,
Its fringing violets blossom yet,
  The old trees o'er it lean.

The winds so sweet with birch and fern
  A sweeter memory blow;
And there in spring the veeries sing
  The song of long ago.

And still the pines of Ramoth wood
  Are moaning like the sea, —
The moaning of the sea of change
  Between myself and thee!

MAY

1

Joseph Addison, 1672; Wellington, 1769.

NATURE'S mighty miracle is still over and around us; and hence awe, wonder, and reverence remain to be the inheritance of humanity.
THE AGENCY OF EVIL.

THE vales shall laugh in flowers, the woods
Grow misty green with leafing buds,
And violets and wind-flowers sway,
Against the throbbing heart of May.
THE CLEAR VISION.

2

J. G. Palfrey, 1796.

THE seasons went
Their rounds, and somewhat to his spirit lent
Of their own calm and measureless content.

Glad even to tears, he heard the robin sing
His song of welcome to the Western spring,
And bluebird borrowing from the sky his wing.
THE PENNSYLVANIA PILGRIM.

3

Nicolò Macchiavelli, 1469.

THE harp at Nature's advent strung
Has never ceased to play;

MAY

The song the stars of morning sung
  Has never died away.

The green earth sends her incense up
  From many a mountain shrine;
From folded leaf and dewy cup
  She pours her sacred wine.

The blue sky is the temple's arch,
  Its transept earth and air,
The music of its starry march
  The chorus of a prayer.

So Nature keeps the reverent frame
  With which her years began,
And all her signs and voices shame
  The prayerless heart of man.
                    THE WORSHIP OF NATURE.

4

J. J. Audubon, 1780; W. H. Prescott, 1796; T. H. Huxley, 1825.

I DIMLY guess from blessings known
  Of greater out of sight,
And, with the chastened Psalmist, own
  His judgments too are right.

I know not what the future hath
  Of marvel or surprise,
Assured alone that life and death
  His mercy underlies.
               THE ETERNAL GOODNESS.

MAY

5

Empress Eugénie, 1826.

LET me find in Thy employ
Peace that dearer is than joy;
Out of self to love be led
And to heaven acclimated,
Until all things sweet and good
Seem my natural habitude!
ANDREW RYKMAN'S PRAYER.

6

HIS light shines on me from above,
  His low voice speaks within, —
The patience of immortal love
  Outwearying mortal sin.

Not mindless of the growing years
  Of care and loss and pain,
My eyes are wet with thankful tears
  For blessings which remain.

If dim the gold of life has grown,
  I will not count it dross,
Nor turn from treasures still my own
  To sigh for lack and loss.
MY BIRTHDAY.

MAY

7

Robert Browning, 1812; Johannes Brahms, 1833.

Not by the page word-painted
Let life be banned or sainted:
Deeper than written scroll
The colors of the soul.

Sweeter than any sung
My songs that found no tongue;
Nobler than any fact
My wish that failed of act.
My Triumph.

8

O Golden Age, whose light is of the dawn,
And not of sunset, forward, not behind,
Flood the new heavens and earth, and with thee
    bring
All the old virtues, whatsoever things
Are pure and honest and of good repute,
But add thereto whatever bard has sung
Or seer has told of when in trance and dream
They saw the Happy Isles of prophecy!
Let Justice hold her scale, and Truth divide
Between the right and wrong; but give the heart
The freedom of its fair inheritance.
Prelude to Among the Hills.

MAY

9

John Brown, 1800.

PERISH with him the folly that seeks through evil good!
Long live the generous purpose unstained with human blood!
Not the raid of midnight terror, but the thought which underlies;
Not the borderer's pride of daring, but the Christian's sacrifice.

BROWN OF OSSAWATOMIE.

10

Jared Sparks, 1789.

WHY idly seek from outward things,
The answer inward silence brings?
Why stretch beyond our proper sphere
And age, for that which lies so near?
Why climb the far-off hills with pain,
A nearer view of heaven to gain?
In lowliest depths of bosky dells
The hermit Contemplation dwells.
A fountain's pine-hung slope his seat,
And lotus-twined his silent feet,
Whence, piercing heaven, with screenèd sight,
He sees at noon the stars, whose light
Shall glorify the coming night.

QUESTIONS OF LIFE.

MAY

11

J. L. Gérôme, 1824.

However full, with something more
  We fain the bag would cram;
We sigh above our crowded nets
  For fish that never swam.

No bounty of indulgent Heaven
  The vague desire can stay;
Self-love is still a Tartar mill
  For grinding prayers alway.
                    The Common Question.

12

Justus von Liebig, 1803; D. G. Rossetti, 1828.

No perfect whole can our nature make;
Here or there the circle will break;
The orb of life as it takes the light
On one side, leaves the other in night.
Never was saint so good and great
As to give no chance at St. Peter's gate
For the plea of the Devil's advocate.
                    The Preacher.

13

Alphonse Daudet, 1840; Arthur Sullivan, 1842.

We gird us bravely to rebuke
  Our erring brother in the wrong,—

MAY

And in the ear of Pride and Power
Our warning voice is strong.

Easier to smite with Peter's sword
Than "watch one hour" in humbling prayer.
Life's "great things," like the Syrian lord,
Our hearts can do and dare.
THE CYPRESS-TREE OF CEYLON.

14

Dante, 1265.

THE song whose thunderous chime
Eternal echoes render, —
The mournful Tuscan's haunted rhyme,
And Milton's starry splendor!
BURNS.

THOU hast midst Life's empty noises
Heard the solemn steps of Time,
And the low mysterious voices
Of another clime.

All the mystery of Being
Hath upon thy spirit pressed, —
Thoughts which, like the Deluge wanderer,
Find no place of rest.
TO —.

MAY

15

M. W. Balfe, 1808; Montalembert, 1810.

SWEET in the fresh green meadows
Sparrow and blackbird sung;
Above him their tinted petals
The blossoming orchards hung.

Around on the wonderful glory
The minister looked and smiled;
"How good is the Lord who gives us
These gifts from His hand, my child!

"Behold in the bloom of apples
And the violets in the sward
A hint of the old, lost beauty
Of the Garden of the Lord!"
THE MINISTER'S DAUGHTER.

16

W. H. Seward, 1801.

NATURE is not solitude:
She crowds us with her thronging wood;
Her many hands reach out to us,
Her many tongues are garrulous;
Perpetual riddles of surprise
She offers to our ears and eyes.
THE MEETING.

MAY

17

Edward Jenner, 1749.

OVER the woods and meadow-lands
A crimson-tinted shadow lay
Of clouds through which the setting day
Flung a slant glory far away.
It glittered on the wet sea-sands,
It flamed upon the city's panes,
Smote the white sails of ships that wore
Outward or in, and glided o'er
The steeples with their veering vanes!

THE PREACHER.

18

John Wilson, 1785.

STILL sits the school-house by the road,
A ragged beggar sleeping;
Around it still the sumachs grow,
And blackberry-vines are creeping.

Within, the master's desk is seen,
Deep scarred by raps official;
The warping floor, the battered seats,
The jack-knife's carved initial;

The charcoal frescos on its wall;
Its door's worn sill, betraying
The feet that, creeping slow to school,
Went storming out to playing!

IN SCHOOL-DAYS.

MAY

19

O FOR boyhood's painless play,
Sleep that wakes in laughing day,
Health that mocks the doctor's rules,
Knowledge never learned of schools,
Of the wild bee's morning chase,
Of the wild-flower's time and place,
Flight of fowl and habitude
Of the tenants of the wood;
How the tortoise bears his shell,
How the woodchuck digs his cell,
And the ground-mole sinks his well;
How the robin feeds her young,
How the oriole's nest is hung;
Where the whitest lilies blow,
Where the freshest berries grow!
THE BAREFOOT BOY.

20

Balzac, 1799; John Stuart Mill, 1806.

THE years no charm from Nature take;
  As sweet her voices call,
As beautiful her mornings break,
  As fair her evenings fall.

Love watches o'er my quiet ways,
  Kind voices speak my name,
And lips that find it hard to praise
  Are slow, at least, to blame.

MAY

How softly ebb the tides of will!
How fields, once lost or won,
Now lie behind me green and still
Beneath a level sun!
MY BIRTHDAY.

21

Elizabeth Fry, 1780.

To melt the hearts that harshness turned to stone
The sweet persuasion of her lips sufficed.
And guilt, which only hate and fear had known,
Saw in her own the pitying love of Christ.

So wheresoe'er the guiding Spirit went
   She followed, finding every prison cell
It opened for her sacred as a tent
   Pitched by Gennesaret or by Jacob's well.

And Pride and Fashion felt her strong appeal,
   And priest and ruler marvelled as they saw
How hand in hand went wisdom with her zeal,
   And woman's pity kept the bounds of law.
THE TWO ELIZABETHS.

22

Richard Wagner, 1813.

WHAT sings the brook? What oracle
Is in the pine-tree's organ swell?

MAY

What may the wind's low burden be?
The meaning of the moaning sea?
The hieroglyphics of the stars?
Or clouded sunset's crimson bars?
I vainly ask, for mocks my skill
The trick of Nature's cipher still.
QUESTIONS OF LIFE.

23

Thomas Hood, 1799; Margaret Fuller, 1810.

HOOD, under all his whims and oddities, conceals the vehement intensity of a reformer. The iron of the world's wrongs had entered into his soul; there is an undertone of sorrow in his lyrics.
MIRTH AND MEDICINE.

24

Queen Victoria, 1819.

"THICKER than water," in one rill
    Through centuries of story
Our Saxon blood has flowed, and still
We share with you its good and ill,
    The shadow and the glory.
TO ENGLISHMEN.

MAY

25

Ralph Waldo Emerson, 1803.

THE mists above the morning rills
Rise white as wings of prayer;
The altar-curtains of the hills
Are sunset's purple air.

The winds with hymns of praise are loud,
Or low with sobs of pain, —
The thunder-organ of the cloud,
The dropping tears of rain.

With drooping head and branches crossed
The twilight forest grieves,
Or speaks with tongues of Pentecost
From all its sunlit leaves.
THE WORSHIP OF NATURE.

26

HE findeth not who seeks his own,
The soul is lost that 's saved alone.
Not on one favored forehead fell
Of old the fire-tongued miracle,
But flamed o'er all the thronging host
The baptism of the Holy Ghost;
Heart answers heart: in one desire
The blending lines of prayer aspire.
" Where in my name, meet two or three,"
Our Lord hath said, " I there will be ! "
THE MEETING.

MAY

27

Julia Ward Howe, 1819.

IF it is not permitted us to believe all things, we can at least hope them. Despair is infidelity and death. Temporally and spiritually, the declaration of inspiration holds good, — "*We are saved by hope.*"

UTOPIAN SCHEMES.

•

REJOICE in hope! The day and night
  Are one with God, and one with them
  Who see by faith the cloudy hem
Of Judgment fringed with Mercy's light!

ASTRÆA AT THE CAPITOL.

28

Thomas Moore, 1779; Louis Agassiz, 1807.

SAID the Master to the youth:
"We have come in search of truth,
  Trying with uncertain key
  Door by door of mystery;
We are reaching, through His laws,
To the garment-hem of Cause. . . .
  As with fingers of the blind,
  We are groping here to find
What the hieroglyphics mean
Of the Unseen in the seen,
What the Thought which underlies

MAY

Nature's masking and disguise,
What it is that hides beneath
Blight and bloom and birth and death.
                THE PRAYER OF AGASSIZ.

29

Patrick Henry, 1736.

DEAR friends still toiling in the sun, —
Ye dearer ones who, gone before,
Are watching from the eternal shore
The slow work by your hands begun, —

Rejoice with me! The chastening rod
Blossoms with love; the furnace heat
Grows cool beneath His blessed feet
Whose form is as the Son of God!
                ASTRÆA AT THE CAPITOL.

30

Decoration Day.

OUR voices take a sober tone, . . .
And innocent mirth is chastened for the sake
Of the brave hearts that never more shall beat,
The eyes that smile no more, the unreturning feet!
                TO S. E. S. AND H. W. S.

MAY

IF, for the age to come, this hour
Of trial hath vicarious power,
And, blest by Thee, our present pain
Be liberty's eternal gain,
    Thy will be done!
                    THY WILL BE DONE.

31

John A. Andrew, 1818.

HE has done the work of a true man, —
    Crown him, honor him, love him.
Weep over him, tears of woman,
    Stoop manliest brows above him!

No duty could overtask him,
    No need his will outrun;
Or ever our lips could ask him,
    His hands the work had done.
                    To G. L. S.

June

JUNE ON THE MERRIMAC

O DWELLERS in the stately towns,
   What come ye out to see?
This common earth, this common sky,
   This water flowing free?

As gayly as these kalmia flowers
   Your door-yard blossoms spring;
As sweetly as these wild wood birds
   Your cagèd minstrels sing.

You find but common bloom and green,
   The rippling river's rune,
The beauty which is everywhere
   Beneath the skies of June.

.   .   .   .

From ceilèd rooms, from silent books,
   From crowded car and town,
Dear Mother Earth, upon thy lap,
   We lay our tired heads down.

Cool, summer wind, our heated brows;
   Blue river, through the green
Of clustering pines, refresh the eyes
   Which all too much have seen.

JUNE

For us these pleasant woodland ways
    Are thronged with memories old,
Have felt the grasp of friendly hands
    And heard love's story told.

A sacred presence overbroods
    The earth whereon we meet;
These winding forest-paths are trod
    By more than mortal feet.

Old friends called from us by the voice
    Which they alone could hear,
From mystery to mystery,
    From life to life, draw near.

More closely for the sake of them
    Each other's hands we press;
Our voices take from them a tone
    Of deeper tenderness.

Our joy is theirs, their trust is ours,
    Alike below, above,
Or here or there, about us fold
    The arms of one great love!

JUNE

1

A YEAR has gone, as the tortoise goes,
    Heavy and slow;
And the same rose blows, and the same sun glows,
    And the same brook sings of a year ago.

There's the same sweet-clover smell in the breeze;
    And the June sun warm
Tangles his wings of fire in the trees,
    Setting, as then, over Fernside farm.
                          TELLING THE BEES.

2

John Randolph, 1773; Thomas Hardy, 1840.

BARD, Sage, and Tribune! in himself
    All moods of mind contrasting, —
The tenderest wail of human woe,
    The scorn like lightning blasting;
The pathos which from rival eyes
    Unwilling tears could summon,
The stinging taunt, the fiery burst
    Of hatred scarcely human!

Mirth, sparkling like a diamond shower,
    From lips of life-long sadness;
Clear picturings of majestic thought
    Upon a ground of madness;
And over all Romance and Song
    A classic beauty throwing,

JUNE

And laurelled Clio at his side
Her storied pages showing.
RANDOLPH OF ROANOKE.

3

Richard Cobden, 1804; Henry James, Sr., 1811.

WHERE our duty's task is wrought
In unison with God's great thought,
The near and future blend in one,
And whatsoe'er is willed, is done!

And ours the grateful service whence
Comes, day by day, the recompense;
The hope, the trust, the purpose stayed,
The fountain and the noonday shade.
SEED-TIME AND HARVEST.

4

O FOR boyhood's time of June,
Crowding years in one brief moon,
When all things I heard or saw,
Me, their master, waited for.
I was rich in flowers and trees,
Humming-birds and honey-bees. . . .
Laughed the brook for my delight
Through the day and through the night,
Whispering at the garden wall,
Talked with me from fall to fall;

JUNE

Mine the sand-rimmed pickerel pond,
Mine the walnut slopes beyond,
Mine, on bending orchard trees,
Apples of Hesperides !
THE BAREFOOT BOY.

5

Adam Smith, 1723.

O, WELCOME calm of heart and mind !
As falls yon fir-tree's loosened rind
To leave a tenderer growth behind,

So fall the weary years away;
A child again, my head I lay
Upon the lap of this sweet day.
SUMMER BY THE LAKESIDE.

6

Nathan Hale, 1755; William Francis Bartlett, 1840.

As Galahad pure, as Merlin sage,
  What worthier knight was found
To grace in Arthur's golden age
  The fabled Table Round?

A voice, the battle's trumpet-note,
  To welcome and restore;
A hand, that all unwilling smote,
  To heal and build once more !

JUNE

A soul of fire, a tender heart
Too warm for hate, he knew
The generous victor's graceful part
To sheathe the sword he drew.
WILLIAM FRANCIS BARTLETT.

7

CARE, that kills the cat, may plough
Wrinkles in the miser's brow,
Deepen envy's spiteful frown,
Draw the mouths of bigots down,
Plague ambition's dream, and sit
Heavy on the hypocrite.
Seldom comes that evil guest
Where the conscience lies at rest,
And brown health and quiet wit
Smiling on the threshold sit.
TO MY OLD SCHOOLMASTER.

8

Charles Reade, 1814; J. E. Millais, 1829.

"MORE wise," she said, "than those who swarm
Our hills in middle summer,
She came, when June's first roses blow,
To greet the early comer.

"Her step grew firmer on the hills
That watch our homesteads over;
On cheek and lip, from summer fields,
She caught the bloom of clover.

JUNE

" For health comes sparkling in the streams
From cool Chocorua stealing :
There 's iron in our Northern winds ;
Our pines are trees of healing."
AMONG THE HILLS.

9

George Stephenson, 1781 ; John Howard Payne, 1791.

THE hills are dearest which our childish feet
Have climbed the earliest; and the streams most
    sweet
Are ever those at which our young lips drank,
Stooped to their waters o'er the grassy bank :

Midst the cold dreary sea-watch, Home's hearth-
    light
Shines round the helmsman plunging through the
    night ;
And still, with inward eye, the traveller sees
In close, dark, stranger streets his native trees.
THE BRIDAL OF PENNACOOK.

10

SING soft, sing low, our lowland river,
    Under thy banks of laurel bloom ;
Softly and sweet, as the hour beseemeth,
    Sing us the songs of peace and home.

JUNE

But to Him who gives us beauty for ashes,
And the oil of joy for mourning long,
Let thy hills give thanks, and all thy waters
Break into jubilant waves of song!

Bring us the air of hills and forests,
The sweet aroma of birch and pine,
Give us a waft of the north-wind laden
With sweetbrier odors and breath of kine!
REVISITED (1865).

11

Ben Jonson, 1574; George Wither, 1588.

O POET rare and old!
Thy words are prophecies;
Forward the age of gold,
The new Saturnian lies.

The universal prayer
And hope are not in vain;
Rise, brothers! and prepare
The way for Saturn's reign.
ASTRÆA.

12

Charles Kingsley, 1819.

RING, bells in unreared steeples,
The joy of unborn peoples!

JUNE

Sound, trumpets far off blown,
Your triumph is my own!

Parcel and part of all,
I keep the festival,
Fore-reach the good to be,
And share the victory.
My Triumph.

13

Madame d'Arblay, 1752 ; Thomas Arnold, 1795.

No longer forward nor behind
  I look in hope or fear;
But, grateful, take the good I find,
  The best of now and here.

I plough no more a desert land,
  To harvest weed and tare;
The manna dropping from God's hand
  Rebukes my painful care.

I break my pilgrim staff, I lay
  Aside the toiling oar;
The angel sought so far away
  I welcome at my door.
My Psalm.

JUNE

14

Harriet Beecher Stowe, 1811.

To her whose vigorous pencil-strokes
Sketched into life her Oldtown Folks;
Whose fireside stories, grave or gay,
In quaint Sam Lawson's vagrant way,
With old New England's flavor rife,
Waifs from her rude idyllic life,
Are racy as the legends old
By Chaucer or Boccaccio told; . .
To her, who world-wide entrance gave
To the log-cabin of the slave,
Made all his want and sorrow known,
And all earth's languages his own.
A Greeting.

15

Magna Charta, signed 1215.

O Englishmen! — in hope and creed,
  In blood and tongue our brothers!
We, too, are heirs of Runnymede;
And Shakespeare's fame and Cromwell's deed
  Are not alone our mother's.
To Englishmen.

16

The birds are glad; the brier-rose fills
The air with sweetness; all the hills

JUNE

Stretch green to June's unclouded sky;
But still I wait with ear and eye
For something gone which should be nigh,
A loss in all familiar things,
In flower that blooms, and bird that sings.
And yet, dear heart! remembering thee,
    Am I not richer than of old?
Safe in thy immortality,
    What change can reach the wealth I hold?
    What chance can mar the pearl and gold
Thy love hath left in trust with me?
Snow-Bound.

17

John Wesley, 1703; Battle of Bunker Hill, 1775.

No Berserk thirst of blood had they,
    No battle-joy was theirs, who set
    Against the alien bayonet
Their homespun breasts in that old day.

Their feet had trodden peaceful ways;
    They loved not strife, they dreaded pain;
    They saw not, what to us is plain,
That God would make man's wrath His praise.

No seers were they, but simple men;
    Its vast results the future hid:
    The meaning of the work they did
Was strange and dark and doubtful then.
Lexington.

JUNE

18

Battle of Waterloo, 1815.

STILL, when the sun of summer burns,
My longing for the hills returns;
And northward, leaving at my back
The warm vale of the Merrimac,
I go to meet the winds of morn,
Blown down the hill-gaps, mountain-born,
Breathe scent of pines, and satisfy
The hunger of a lowland eye.
     A SUMMER PILGRIMAGE.

19

Confucius, 551 B. C.; Pascal, 1623.

TRUTH is one;
And, in all lands beneath the sun,
Whoso hath eyes to see may see
The tokens of its unity. . .
The angels to our Aryan sires
Talked by the earliest houschold fires;
The prophets of the elder day,
The slant-eyed sages of Cathay,
Read not the riddle all amiss
Of higher life evolved from this.
     MIRIAM.

JUNE

20

Anna Letitia Barbauld, 1743.

AND not in vain in this soft air
Shall hard-strung nerves relax,
Not all in vain the o'erworn brain
Forego its daily tax.

Unheeded let the newsboy call,
Aside the ledger lay:
The world will keep its treadmill step
Though we fall out to-day.

The truants of life's weary school,
Without excuse from thrift
We change for once the gains of toil
For God's unpurchased gift.
JUNE ON THE MERRIMAC.

21

Bishop Stubbs, 1825.

O FEARFUL heart and troubled brain!
Take hope and strength from this,
That Nature never hints in vain,
Nor prophesies amiss.

Her wild birds sing the same sweet stave,
Her lights and airs are given
Alike to playground and the grave;
And over both is Heaven.
THE OLD BURYING-GROUND.

JUNE

22

Thomas Day, 1748; Giuseppe Mazzini, 1805.

O YOUTH and Beauty, loved of all!
  Ye pass from girlhood's gate of dreams;
In broader ways your footsteps fall,
  Ye test the truth of all that seems.

Give and receive; go forth and bless
  The world that needs the hand and heart
Of Martha's helpful carefulness
  No less than Mary's better part.
                                AT SCHOOL-CLOSE.

23

Midsummer Eve; F. O. C. Darley, 1822.

AWAY with weary cares and themes!
Swing wide the moonlit gate of dreams!
Leave free once more the land which teems
  With wonders and romances!
Where thou, with clear discerning eyes,
Shalt rightly read the truth which lies
Beneath the quaintly masking guise
  Of wild and wizard fancies.

Lo! once again our feet we set
On still green wood-paths, twilight wet,
By lonely brooks, whose waters fret
  The roots of spectral beeches;

JUNE

Again the hearth-fire glimmers o'er
Home's whitewashed wall and painted floor,
And young eyes widening to the lore
Of faery-folks and witches.
To My Sister.

24

St. John Baptist; John Hampden died, 1643.

THE English revolution of the seventeenth century was prodigal in the development of the real nobility of the mind and heart. Its history is bright with the footprints of men whose very names still stir the hearts of freemen, the world over, like a trumpet peal. Say what we may of its fanaticism, laugh as we may at its extravagant enjoyment of newly acquired religious and civil liberty, who shall now venture to deny that it was the golden age of England?
John Bunyan.

25

O FOR festal dainties spread,
Like my bowl of milk and bread;
Pewter spoon and bowl of wood,
On the doorstone, gray and rude!
O'er me, like a regal tent,
Cloudy-ribbed, the sunset bent,
Purple-curtained, fringed with gold,
Looped in many a wind-swung fold;

JUNE

While for music came the play
Of the pied frogs' orchestra;
And, to light the noisy choir,
Lit the fly his lamp of fire.
I was monarch : pomp and joy
Waited on the barefoot boy!
THE BAREFOOT BOY.

26

Philip Doddridge, 1702.

THE gray sky wears again its gold
    And purple of adorning,
And manhood's noonday shadows hold
    The dews of boyhood's morning.

The dews that washed the dust and soil
    From off the wings of pleasure,
The sky, that flecked the ground of toil
    With golden threads of leisure.
BURNS.

27

Sir William Pepperrell, 1696.

STILL waits kind Nature to impart
    Her choicest gifts to such as gain
An entrance to her loving heart
    Through the sharp discipline of pain.

JUNE

Forever from the Hand that takes
One blessing from us others fall;
And, soon or late, our Father makes
His perfect recompense to all!
SUMMER BY THE LAKESIDE.

28

Jean Jacques Rousseau, 1712.

UNTROD by him the path he showed,
Sweet pictures on his easel glowed
Of simple faith, and loves of home,
And virtue's golden days to come.

But weakness, shame, and folly made
The foil to all his pen portrayed;
Still, where his dreamy splendors shone,
The shadow of himself was thrown.
THE CHAPEL OF THE HERMITS.

29

St. Peter; Rubens, 1577; Celia Thaxter, 1835.

THE letter fails, and systems fall,
   And every symbol wanes;
The Spirit over-brooding all
   Eternal Love remains.

And not for signs in heaven above
   Or earth below they look,

JUNE

Who know with John His smile of love,
With Peter His rebuke.

In joy of inward peace, or sense
  Of sorrow over sin,
He is His own best evidence,
  His witness is within.
Our Master.

30

Horace Vernet, 1789.

Did not the gifts of sun and air
To good and ill alike declare
The all-compassionate Father's care?

In the white soul that stooped to raise
The lost one from her evil ways,
Thou saw'st the Christ, whom angels praise!

A bodiless Divinity,
The still small Voice that spake to thee
Was the Holy Spirit's mystery!

Revealed in love and sacrifice,
The Holiest passed before thine eyes,
One and the same, in threefold guise.

The equal Father in rain and sun,
His Christ in the good to evil done,
His Voice in thy soul; — and the Three are One!
Trinitas.

July

SUMMER BY THE LAKESIDE

WHITE clouds, whose shadows haunt the deep,
Light mists, whose soft embraces keep
The sunshine on the hills asleep!

O isles of calm! O dark, still wood!
And stiller skies that overbrood
Your rest with deeper quietude!

O shapes and hues, dim beckoning, through
Yon mountain gaps, my longing view
Beyond the purple and the blue,

To stiller sea and greener land,
And softer lights and airs more bland,
And skies, — the hollow of God's hand!

Transfused through you, O mountain friends!
With mine your solemn spirit blends,
And life no more hath separate ends.

I read each misty mountain sign,
I know the voice of wave and pine,
And I am yours, and ye are mine.

Life's burdens fall, its discords cease,
I lapse into the glad release
Of Nature's own exceeding peace.

JULY

1

I CALL to mind the summer day,
  The early harvest mowing,
The sky with sun and clouds at play,
  And flowers with breezes blowing.

I hear the blackbird in the corn,
  The locust in the haying;
And, like the fabled hunter's horn,
  Old tunes my heart is playing.
                                BURNS.

2

Marston Moor, 1644.

THEN Freedom sternly said: "I shun
No strife nor pang beneath the sun,
When human rights are staked and won.

"I knelt with Ziska's hunted flock,
I watched in Toussaint's cell of rock,
I walked with Sidney to the block.

"The moor of Marston felt my tread,
Through Jersey snows the march I led,
My voice Magenta's charges sped."
                           THE WATCHERS.

JULY

3

John Singleton Copley, 1737.

For art and labor met in truce,
For beauty made the bride of use,
We thank Thee; but, withal, we crave
The austere virtues strong to save,
The honor proof to place or gold,
The manhood never bought nor sold!

Oh make Thou us, through centuries long,
In peace secure, in justice strong;
Around our gift of freedom draw
The safeguards of Thy righteous law;
And, cast in some diviner mould,
Let the new cycle shame the old!
Centennial Hymn.

4

Independence Day; Nathaniel Hawthorne, 1804; Garibaldi, 1807.

We give thy natal day to hope,
  O Country of our love and prayer!
Thy way is down no fatal slope,
  But up to freer sun and air.

Tried as by furnace-fires, and yet
  By God's grace only stronger made,
In future tasks before thee set
  Thou shalt not lack the old-time aid.

. . . .

JULY

With peace that comes of purity
And strength to simple justice due,
So runs our loyal dream of thee;
God of our fathers! — make it true.
OUR COUNTRY.

5

D. G. Farragut, 1801; "George Sand," 1804.

FAIR First-Day mornings, steeped in summer calm,
Warm, tender, restful, sweet with woodland balm,
Came to him, like some mother-hallowed psalm
To the tired grinder at the noisy wheel
Of labor, winding off from memory's reel
A golden thread of music.
THE PENNSYLVANIA PILGRIM.

6

John Huss, 1373; John Flaxman, 1755.

THE path of life we walk to-day
  Is strange as that the Hebrews trod;
We need the shadowing rock, as they, —
  We need, like them, the guides of God.

God send His angels, Cloud and Fire,
  To lead us o'er the desert sand!
God give our hearts their long desire,
  His shadow in a weary land!
"THE ROCK" IN EL GHOR.

JULY

7

GOOD-BY to pain and care ! I take
    Mine ease to-day :
Here where these sunny waters break,
And ripples this keen breeze, I shake
All burdens from the heart, all weary thoughts
    away.

I draw a freer breath — I seem
    Like all I see —
Waves in the sun — the white-winged gleam
Of sea-birds in the slanting beam —
And far-off sails which flit before the south-wind
    free.
HAMPTON BEACH.

8

Fitz-Greene Halleck, 1790.

IN common ways, with common men,
    He served his race and time
As well as if his clerkly pen
    Had never danced to rhyme.

If, in the thronged and noisy mart,
    The Muses found their son,
Could any say his tuneful art
    A duty left undone?
FITZ-GREENE HALLECK.

JULY

9

Henry Hallam, 1777.

AND prayer is made, and praise is given,
  By all things near and far;
The ocean looketh up to heaven,
  And mirrors every star.

Its waves are kneeling on the strand,
  As kneels the human knee,
Their white locks bowing to the sand,
  The priesthood of the sea!

They pour their glittering treasures forth,
  Their gifts of pearl they bring,
And all the listening hills of earth
  Take up the song they sing.
              THE WORSHIP OF NATURE.

10

John Calvin, 1509; Robert Chambers, 1802.

I REVERENCE old-time faith and men,
But God is near us now as then;
His force of love is still unspent,
His hate of sin as imminent;
And still the measure of our needs
Outgrows the cramping bounds of creeds.
              THE MEETING.

JULY

11

John Quincy Adams, 1767.

O FOR the tongue of him who lies at rest
In Quincy's shade of patrimonial trees, —
Last of the Puritan tribunes and the best.
TO KOSSUTH.

HE rests with the immortals; his journey has been long:
For him no wail of sorrow, but a pæan full and strong!
So well and bravely has he done the work he found to do,
To justice, freedom, duty, God, and man forever true.
JOHN QUINCY ADAMS.

12

H. D. Thoreau, 1817.

HIMSELF to Nature's heart so near
That all her voices in his ear
Of beast or bird had meanings clear,
Like Apollonius of old,
Who knew the tales the sparrows told,
Or Hermes who interpreted
What the sage cranes of Nilus said.
SNOW-BOUND.

JULY

13

AND if the husband or the wife
  In home's strong light discovers
Such slight defaults as failed to meet
  The blinded eyes of lovers,

Why need we care to ask?—who dreams
  Without their thorns of roses,
Or wonders that the truest steel
  The readiest spark discloses?

For still in mutual sufferance lies
  The secret of true living;
Love scarce is love that never knows
  The sweetness of forgiving.
AMONG THE HILLS.

14

John Gibson Lockhart, 1794.

"HANDS that ope but to receive
Empty close; they only live
Richly who can richly give.

"Still," she sighed, with moistening eyes,
"Love is sweet in any guise;
But its best is sacrifice!

"He who, giving, does not crave
  Likest is to Him who gave
Life itself the loved to save.

JULY

"Love, that self-forgetful gives,
Sows surprise of ripened sheaves,
Late or soon its own receives."
THE TWO LOVES.

15

Rembrandt, 1606.

THEY sat and watched in idle mood
The gleam and shade of lake and wood, —
The beach the keen light smote,
The white sail of a boat, —

Swan flocks of lilies shoreward lying,
In sweetness, not in music, dying, —
Hardhack, and virgin's-bower,
And white-spiked clethra-flower.
THE MAIDS OF ATTITASH.

16

Sir Joshua Reynolds, 1723.

THE Beauty which old Greece or Rome
Sung, painted, wrought, lies close at home;
We need but eye and ear
In all our daily walks to trace
The outlines of incarnate grace,
The hymns of gods to hear!
To ——.

JULY

17

Isaac Watts, 1674.

SOMETIMES comes to soul and sense
The feeling which is evidence
That very near about us lies
The realm of spiritual mysteries.
The sphere of the supernal powers
Impinges on this world of ours.
The breath of a diviner air
Blows down the answer of a prayer. . . .
With smile of trust and folded hands,
The passive soul in waiting stands
To feel, as flowers the sun and dew,
The One true Life its own renew.

THE MEETING.

18

George Fox, 1624; Gilbert White, 1720; W. M. Thackeray, 1811.

O BEAUTY, old yet ever new!
Eternal Voice, and Inward Word,
The Logos of the Greek and Jew,
The old sphere-music which the Samian heard!

Truth which the sage and prophet saw,
Long sought without, but found within,
The Law of Love beyond all law,
The Life o'erflooding mortal death and sin!

JULY

Shine on us with the light which glowed
    Upon the trance-bound shepherd's way,
Who saw the Darkness overflowed
    And drowned by tides of everlasting Day.
THE SHADOW AND THE LIGHT.

19

A STRANGER now, a world-worn man,
    Is he who bears my name;
But thou, methinks, whose mortal life
    Immortal youth became,
    Art evermore the same.

Thou art not here, thou art not there,
    Thy place I cannot see;
I only know that where thou art
    The blessed angels be,
    And heaven is glad for thee.

. . . .

Look forth once more through space and time,
    And let thy sweet shade fall
In tenderest grace of soul and form
    On memory's frescoed wall.
    A shadow, and yet all!
A SEA DREAM.

20

John Sterling, 1806.

METHINKS the spirit's temper grows
    Too soft in this still air;

JULY

Somewhat the restful heart foregoes
  Of needed watch and prayer.

The bark by tempest vainly tossed
  May founder in the calm,
And he who braved the polar frost
  Faint by the isles of balm.
                    MY BIRTHDAY.

21

Robert Burns died, 1796.

TO-DAY be every fault forgiven
  Of him in whom we joy!
We take, with thanks, the gold of Heaven
  And leave the earth's alloy.
Be ours his music as of spring,
  His sweetness as of flowers,
The songs the bard himself might sing
  In holier ears than ours.
                    THE MEMORY OF BURNS.

22

WHEN heats as of a tropic clime
  Burned all our inland valleys through,
Three friends, the guests of summer time,
  Pitched their white tent where sea-winds blew.
Behind them, marshes, seamed and crossed
With narrow creeks, and flower-embossed,

JULY

Stretched to the dark oak wood, whose leafy arms
Screened from the stormy East the pleasant inland
farms.

They rested there, escaped awhile
  From cares that wear the life away,
To eat the lotus of the Nile
  And drink the poppies of Cathay, —
To fling their loads of custom down,
Like drift-weed, on the sand-slopes brown,
And in the sea-waves drown the restless pack
Of duties, claims, and needs that barked upon their
track.
THE TENT ON THE BEACH.

23

Charlotte Cushman, 1816.

OUR common Master did not pen
His followers up from other men; . . .
His sermons were the healthful talk
That shorter made the mountain-walk,
His wayside texts were flowers and birds,
Where mingled with His gracious words
The rustle of the tamarisk-tree
And ripple-wash of Galilee.
THE MEETING.

JULY

24

Alexandre Dumas, 1803.

WHAT heed I of the dusty land
  And noisy town?
I see the mighty deep expand
From its white line of glimmering sand
To where the blue of heaven on bluer waves shuts
  down!

In listless quietude of mind,
  I yield to all
The change of cloud and wave and wind
And passive on the flood reclined,
I wander with the waves, and with them rise and
  fall.

HAMPTON BEACH.

25

St. James.

WE live by Faith; but Faith is not the slave
  Of text and legend. Reason's voice and God's,
  Nature's and Duty's, never are at odds.
What asks our Father of His children, save
Justice and mercy and humility,
  A reasonable service of good deeds,
  Pure living, tenderness to human needs,
Reverence and trust, and prayer for light to see

JULY

The Master's footprints in our daily ways?
  No knotted scourge nor sacrificial knife,
  But the calm beauty of an ordered life
Whose very breathing is unworded praise! —
A life that stands as all true lives have stood,
Firm-rooted in the faith that God is Good.
REQUIREMENT.

26

Winthrop Mackworth Praed, 1802.

THANKS for thy gift
  Of ocean flowers,
 Born where the golden drift
 Of the slant sunshine falls
 Down the green, tremulous walls
Of water, to the cool still coral bowers,
Where, under rainbows of perpetual showers,
  God's gardens of the deep
  His patient angels keep;
Gladdening the dim, strange solitude
 With fairest forms and hues.
TO AVIS KEENE.
[On Receiving a Basket of Sea-Mosses.]

27

Thomas Campbell, 1777; Atlantic Telegraph completed, 1866.

FROM world to world his couriers fly,
  Thought-winged and shod with fire;
 The angel of His stormy sky
  Rides down the sunken wire.

JULY

Weave on, swift shuttle of the Lord,
  Beneath the deep so far,
The bridal robe of earth's accord,
  The funeral shroud of war!

For lo! the fall of Ocean's wall
  Space mocked and time outrun;
And round the world the thought of all
  Is as the thought of one!
                              THE CABLE HYMN.

28

Alexandre Dumas, the Younger, 1824.

NEED has its rights, necessity its claim.
Yea, even self-wrought misery and shame
Test well the charity suffering long and kind.
The home-pressed question of the age can find
No answer in the catch-words of the blind
Leaders of blind. Solution there is none
Save in the Golden Rule of Christ alone.
                              THE PROBLEM.

29

Alexis de Tocqueville, 1805.

ROCKED on her breast, these pines and I
Alike on Nature's love rely;
And equal seems to live or die.

JULY

Assured that He whose presence fills
With light the spaces of these hills
No evil to His creatures wills,

The simple faith remains, that He
Will do, whatever that may be,
The best alike for man and tree.

What mosses over one shall grow,
What light and life the other know,
Unanxious, leaving Him to show.
Summer by the Lakeside.

30

Samuel Rogers, 1763.

Drop Thy still dews of quietness,
  Till all our strivings cease;
Take from our souls the strain and stress,
And let our ordered lives confess
  The beauty of Thy peace.

Breathe through the heats of our desire
  Thy coolness and Thy balm;
Let sense be dumb, let flesh retire;
Speak through the earthquake, wind, and fire,
  O still, small voice of calm!
The Brewing of Soma.

JULY

31

George Henry Thomas, 1816.

AND light is mingled with the gloom,
    And joy with grief;
Divinest compensations come,
Through thorns of judgment mercies bloom
    In sweet relief.

Who murmurs that in these dark days
    His lot is cast?
God's hand within the shadow lays
The stones whereon His gates of praise
    Shall rise at last.

Turn and o'erturn, O outstretched Hand!
    Nor stint, nor stay;
The years have never dropped their sand
On mortal issue vast and grand
    As ours to-day.

ANNIVERSARY POEM (1863).

August

PRELUDE TO AMONG THE HILLS

ALONG the roadside, like the flowers of gold
That tawny Incas for their gardens wrought,
Heavy with sunshine droops the goldenrod,
And the red pennons of the cardinal flowers
Hang motionless upon their upright staves.
The sky is hot and hazy, and the wind,
Wing-weary with its long flight from the south,
Unfelt; yet, closely scanned, yon maple leaf
With faintest motion, as one stirs in dreams,
Confesses it. The locust by the wall
Stabs the noon-silence with his sharp alarm.
A single hay-cart down the dusty road
Creaks slowly, with its driver fast asleep
On the load's top. Against the neighboring hill,
Huddled along the stone wall's shady side,
The sheep show white, as if a snowdrift still
Defied the dog-star. Through the open door
A drowsy smell of flowers — gray heliotrope,
And white sweet clover, and shy mignonette —
Comes faintly in, and silent chorus lends
To the pervading symphony of peace.

AUGUST

1

Lammas; George Ticknor, 1791; Cavour, 1810.

My ear is full of summer sounds,
  Of summer sights my languid eye;
Beyond the dusty village bounds
I loiter in my daily rounds,
  And in the noontime shadows lie.

I hear the wild bee wind his horn,
  The bird swings on the ripened wheat,
The long green lances of the corn
Are tilting in the winds of morn,
  The locust shrills his song of heat.
                    THE SUMMONS.

2

Joseph Sturge, 1793; E. A. Freeman, 1823; F. Marion Crawford, 1854.

THANKS for the good man's beautiful example,
  Who in the vilest saw
Some sacred crypt or altar of a temple
  Still vocal with God's law;

Not his the golden pen's or lip's persuasion,
  But a fine sense of right,
And Truth's directness, meeting each occasion
  Straight as a line of light.
        IN REMEMBRANCE OF JOSEPH STURGE.

AUGUST

3
Juliana Horatia Ewing, 1841.

OUR sweet illusions only die
Fulfilling love's sure prophecy;
And every wish for better things
An undreamed beauty nearer brings.

For fate is servitor of love;
Desire and hope and longing prove
The secret of immortal youth,
And Nature cheats us into truth.
THE SEEKING OF THE WATERFALL.

4
Percy Bysshe Shelley, 1792; Edward Irving, 1792.

THE glorious ideal of Shelley, who, atheist as he was through early prejudice and defective education, saw the horizon of the world's future kindling with the light of a better day, — that hope and that faith which constitute, as it were, the world's life, and without which it would be dark and dead, cannot be in vain.
THE WORLD'S END.

5
THE clouds, which rise with thunder, slake
Our thirsty souls with rain:
The blow most dreaded falls to break
From off our limbs a chain;

AUGUST

And wrongs of man to man but make
   The love of God more plain.
As through the shadowy lens of even
The eye looks farthest into heaven
On gleams of star and depths of blue
The glaring sunshine never knew!
ALL'S WELL.

6

Fénelon, 1651; Tennyson, 1809.

OH, more than thrice-blest relic, more
Than solemn rite or sacred lore,
The holy life of one who trod
The foot-marks of the Christ of God!

He lived the Truth which reconciled
The strong man Reason, Faith the child;
In him belief and act were one,
The homilies of duty done!
THE CHAPEL OF THE HERMITS.

7

Joseph Rodman Drake, 1795.

AND there, on breezy morns, they saw
   The fishing-schooners outward run,
Their low-bent sails in tack and flaw
   Turned white or dark to shade and sun.

AUGUST

Sometimes, in calms of closing day,
They watched the spectral mirage play,
Saw low, far islands looming tall and nigh,
And ships, with upturned keels, sail like a sea the sky.
THE TENT ON THE BEACH.

8

A GLIMMER of heat was in the air, —
  The dark green woods were still;
And the skirts of a heavy thunder-cloud
  Hung over the western hill.

Black, thick, and vast arose that cloud
  Above the wilderness,
As some dark world from upper air
  Were stooping over this.

At times the solemn thunder pealed,
  And all was still again,
Save a low murmur in the air
  Of coming wind and rain.
THE EXILES.

9

Izaak Walton, 1593; John Dryden, 1631.

Passages
From Izaak Walton's Angler, sweet and fresh
As the flower-skirted streams of Staffordshire,

AUGUST

Where, under aged trees, the southwest wind
Of soft June mornings fanned the thin, white hair
Of the sage fisher.
THE BRIDAL OF PENNACOOK.

10

LIFE shall on and upward go;
  Th' eternal step of Progress beats
To that great anthem, calm and slow,
  Which God repeats.

Take heart! the Waster builds again, —
  A charmèd life old Goodness hath;
The tares may perish, but the grain
  Is not for death.

God works in all things; all obey
  His first propulsion from the night:
Wake thou and watch! the world is gray
  With morning light!
THE REFORMER.

11

Jeffries Wyman, 1814.

WHITE with its sun-bleached dust, the pathway winds
Before me; dust is on the shrunken grass,
And on the trees beneath whose boughs I pass;

AUGUST

Frail screen against the Hunter of the sky,
Who, glaring on me with his lidless eye,
   While mounting with his dog-star high and higher
Ambushed in light intolerable, unbinds
   The burnished quiver of his shafts of fire.
Between me and the hot fields of his South
A tremulous glow, as from a furnace-mouth,
Glimmers and swims before my dazzled sight,
   As if the burning arrows of his ire
Broke as they fell, and shattered into light.
                                      PICTURES.

12

Robert Southey, 1774.

FAINT not, falter not, nor plead
   Thy weakness; truth itself is strong;
The lion's strength, the eagle's speed,
   Are not alone vouchsafed to wrong.

Thy nature, which, through fire and flood,
   To place or gain finds out its way,
Hath power to seek the highest good,
   And duty's holiest call obey!
                                  THE VOICES.

13

FLOWERS spring to blossom where she walks
   The careful ways of duty;
Our hard, stiff lines of life with her
   Are flowing curves of beauty.

AUGUST

Unspoken homilies of peace
    Her daily life is preaching;
The still refreshment of the dew
    Is her unconscious teaching.

Her presence lends its warmth and health
    To all who come before it.
If woman lost us Eden, such
    As she alone restore it.
AMONG THE HILLS.

14

NOT vain the vision which the prophets saw,
Skirting with green the fiery waste of war,
Through the hot sand-gleam, looming soft and calm
On the sky's rim, the fountain-shading palm.
Still lives for Earth, which fiends so long have trod,
The great hope resting on the truth of God, —
Evil shall cease and Violence pass away,
And the tired world breathe free through a long
    Sabbath day.
THE PEACE CONVENTION.

15

Napoleon, 1769; Walter Scott, 1771; Thomas De Quincey, 1785.

HUMAN hearts remain unchanged: the sorrow
    and the sin,
The loves and hopes and fears of old, are to our
    own akin;

AUGUST

And if, in tales our fathers told, the songs our
    mothers sung,
Tradition wears a snowy beard, Romance is always
    young.
MARY GARVIN.

16

Lavoisier, 1743.

On my cheek I feel the western wind,
  And hear it telling to the orchard trees,
  And to the faint and flower-forsaken bees,
  Tales of fair meadows, green with constant
    streams,
And mountains rising blue and cool behind,
  Where in moist dells the purple orchis gleams,
And starred with white the virgin's bower is twined.
So the o'erwearied pilgrim, as he fares
  Along life's summer waste, at times is fanned,
Even at noontide, by the cool, sweet airs
  Of a serener and a holier land,
  Fresh as the morn, and as the dewfall bland.
Breath of the blessed Heaven for which we pray,
Blow from the eternal hills! make glad our earthly
    way!
PICTURES.

AUGUST

17

Fredrika Bremer, 1801.

THY sweet thoughts and northern fancies
  Meet and mingle with our mirth.
And o'er weary spirits keeping
  Sorrow's night-watch, long and chill,
Shine they like thy sun of summer
  Over midnight vale and hill.
                    To FREDRIKA BREMER.

18

T. W. Parsons, 1819; Emperor Francis Joseph, 1830.

ONE, with years grown wiser, said:
" So, always baffled, not misled,
  We follow where before us runs
  The vision of the shining ones.

" Not where they seem their signals fly,
  Their voices while we listen die;
  We cannot keep, however fleet,
  The quick time of their wingèd feet.

" From youth to age unresting stray
  These kindly mockers in our way;
  Yet lead they not, the baffling elves,
  To something better than themselves?"
                    THE SEEKING OF THE WATERFALL.

AUGUST

19

John Woolman, 1720.

EARNEST toil and strong endeavor
Of a spirit which within
Wrestles with familiar evil
And besetting sin ;

And without, with tireless vigor,
  Steady heart, and weapon strong,
In the power of truth assailing
  Every form of wrong.

O'er life's humblest duties throwing
  Light the earthling never knew,
Freshening all its dark waste places
  As with Hermon's dew.

Beauty, such as Goethe pictured,
  Such as Shelley dreamed of, shed
Living warmth and starry brightness
  Round that poor man's head.
                To ——.
    [*With a copy of Woolman's Journal.*]

20

Robert Herrick, 1591.

WITH warning hand I mark Time's rapid flight
From life's glad morning to its solemn night;

AUGUST

Yet, through the dear God's love, I also show
There's Light above me by the Shade below.
INSCRIPTION ON A SUN-DIAL.

21

Jules Michelet, 1798; John Tyndall, 1820.

Now in the west, the heavy clouds
  Scattered and fell asunder,
While feebler came the rush of rain,
  And fainter growled the thunder.

And through the broken clouds, the sun
  Looked out serene and warm,
Painting its holy symbol-light
  Upon the passing storm.

Oh, beautiful! that rainbow span,
  O'er dim Crane-neck was blended ; —
One bright foot touched the eastern hills,
  And one with ocean blended.
THE EXILES.

22

SOMETIMES a cloud, with thunder black,
  Stooped low upon the darkening main,
Piercing the waves along its track
  With the slant javelins of rain.

AUGUST

And when west-wind and sunshine warm
    Chased out to sea its wrecks of storm,
They saw the prismy hues in thin spray showers
Where the green buds of waves burst into white
    froth flowers.
THE TENT ON THE BEACH.

23

Cuvier, 1769.

EARTH'S rocky tablets bear forever
    The dint of rain and small bird's track:
Who knows but that my idle verses
    May leave some trace by Merrimac!

So, when this fluid age we live in
    Shall stiffen round my careless rhyme,
Who made the vagrant tracks may puzzle
    The savans of the coming time:

And, following out their dim suggestions,
    Some idly-curious hand may draw
My doubtful portraiture, as Cuvier
    Drew fish and bird from fin and claw.
THE FIRST FLOWERS.

AUGUST

24

William Wilberforce, 1759.

THE truths ye urge are borne abroad
By every wind and every tide;
The voice of Nature and of God
Speaks out upon your side.

The weapons which your hands have found
Are those which Heaven itself has wrought,
Light, Truth, and Love; your battle-ground
The free, broad field of Thought.
TO THE REFORMERS OF ENGLAND.

25

C. K. J. von Bunsen, 1791; Bret Harte, 1839.

AND when along the line of shore
The mists crept upward chill and damp,
Stretched, careless, on their sandy floor
Beneath the flaring lantern lamp,
They talked of all things old and new,
Read, slept, and dreamed as idlers do;
And in the unquestioned freedom of the tent,
Body and o'er-taxed mind to healthful ease unbent.
THE TENT ON THE BEACH.

AUGUST

26

Sir Robert Walpole, 1676; Prince Albert, 1819.

WE search the world for truth; we cull
The good, the pure, the beautiful,
From graven stone and written scroll,
From all old flower-fields of the soul;
And, weary seekers of the best,
We come back laden from our quest,
To find that all the sages said
Is in the Book our mothers read.
MIRIAM.

27

Hegel, 1770.

AH me! we doubt the shining skies,
   Seen through our shadows of offence,
And drown with our poor childish cries
The cradle-hymn of kindly Providence.

And still we love the evil cause,
   And of the just effect complain:
We tread upon life's broken laws,
And murmur at our self-inflicted pain.
THE SHADOW AND THE LIGHT.

AUGUST

28

John Locke, 1632; Goethe, 1749; Tolstoi, 1828.

THE soul itself its awful witness is.
Say not in evil doing, "No one sees,"
And so offend the conscious One within,
Whose ear can hear the silences of sin
Ere they find voice, whose eyes unsleeping see
The secret motions of iniquity.

Nor in thy folly say, "I am alone."
For, seated in thy heart, as on a throne,
The ancient Judge and Witness liveth still,
To note thy act and thought; and as thy ill
Or good goes from thee, far beyond thy reach,
The solemn Doomsman's seal is set on each.
THE INWARD JUDGE.

29

F. D. Maurice, 1805; O. W. Holmes, 1809.

HIS still the keen analysis
 Of men and moods, electric wit,
Free play of mirth and tenderness
 To heal the slightest wound from it.

And his the pathos touching all
 Life's sins and sorrows and regrets,
Its hopes and fears, its final call
 And rest beneath the violets.

AUGUST

His sparkling surface scarce betrays
The thoughtful tide beneath it rolled,
The wisdom of the latter days,
And tender memories of the old.
OUR AUTOCRAT (1879).

30

CLIMBING a path which leads back never more
We heard behind his footsteps and his cheer;
Now, face to face, we greet him standing here
Upon the lonely summit of Fourscore!
Welcome to us, o'er whom the lengthened day
Is closing and the shadows colder grow,
His genial presence, like an afterglow,
Following the one just vanishing away.
Long be it ere the table shall be set
For the last breakfast of the Autocrat,
And love repeat with smiles and tears thereat
His own sweet songs that time shall not forget.
Waiting with us the call to come up higher,
Life is not less, the heavens are only nigher!
O. W. HOLMES ON HIS EIGHTIETH BIRTHDAY.

31

John Bunyan died, 1688.

THE broad and pleasant "river of the Water of Life" glided peacefully before him, fringed "on either side with green trees, with all manner of fruit," and leaves of healing, with "meadows beau-

AUGUST

tified with lilies, and green all the year long;" he saw the Delectable Mountains, glorious with sunshine, overhung with gardens and orchards and vineyards; and beyond all, the Land of Beulah, with its eternal sunshine, its song of birds, its music of fountains, its purple clustered vines, and groves through which walked the Shining Ones, silver-winged and beautiful.

WHAT were bars and bolts and prison walls to him, whose eyes were anointed to see, and whose ears opened to hear, the glory and the rejoicing of the City of God, when the pilgrims were conducted to its golden gates, from the black and bitter river, with the sounding trumpeters, the transfigured harpers with their crowns of gold, the sweet voices of angels, the welcoming peal of bells in the holy city, and the songs of the redeemed ones?

JOHN BUNYAN.

September

SUNSET ON THE BEARCAMP

A GOLD fringe on the purpling hem
   Of hills the river runs
As down its long green valley falls
   The last of summer's suns.
Along its tawny gravel-bed
   Broad-flowing, swift, and still,
As if its meadow levels felt
   The hurry of the hill,
Noiseless between its banks of green
   From curve to curve it slips;
The drowsy maple-shadows rest
   Like fingers on its lips.

Touched by a light that hath no name,
   A glory never sung,
Aloft on sky and mountain wall
   Are God's great pictures hung.
How changed the summits vast and old!
   No longer granite-browed,
They melt in rosy mist; the rock
   Is softer than the cloud;
The valley holds its breath; no leaf
   Of all its elms is twirled:
The silence of eternity
   Seems falling on the world.

SEPTEMBER

Slow fades the vision of the sky,
  The golden water pales,
And over all the valley-land
  A gray-winged vapor sails.
I go the common way of all;
  The sunset fires will burn,
The flowers will blow, the river flow,
  When I no more return.
No whisper from the mountain pine
  Nor lapsing stream shall tell
The stranger, treading where I tread,
  Of him who loved them well.

But beauty seen is never lost,
  God's colors all are fast;
The glory of this sunset heaven
  Into my soul has passed, —
A sense of gladness unconfined
  To mortal date or clime;
As the soul liveth, it shall live
  Beyond the years of time.
Beside the mystic asphodels
  Shall bloom the home-born flowers,
And new horizons flush and glow
  With sunset hues of ours.

SEPTEMBER

1

L. H. Sigourney, 1791.

SEPTEMBER sunsets, changing forests, moonrise
and cloud, sun and rain, — I for one am contented
with them. They fill my heart with a sense of
beauty.
THE WORLD'S END.

SHE sang alone, ere womanhood had known
  The gift of song which fills the air to-day:
Tender and sweet, a music all her own
  May fitly linger where she knelt to pray.
LYDIA H. SIGOURNEY.
[Inscription in Christ Church, Hartford.]

2

John Howard, 1726.

FRINGING the stream, at every turn
Swung low the waving fronds of fern;
From stony cleft and mossy sod
Pale asters sprang, and goldenrod.

And still the waters sang the sweet,
Glad song that stirred its gliding feet,
And found in rock and root the keys
Of its beguiling melodies.
THE SEEKING OF THE WATERFALL.

SEPTEMBER

3

Mary Whittier Caldwell, 1806.

THERE, too, our elder sister plied
Her evening task the stand beside;
A full, rich nature, free to trust,
Truthful and almost sternly just,
Impulsive, earnest, prompt to act,
And make her generous thought a fact,
Keeping with many a light disguise
The secret of self-sacrifice.
O heart sore-tried! thou hast the best
That Heaven itself could give thee, — rest.
SNOW-BOUND.

4

Phœbe Cary, 1824.

YEARS since (but names to me before),
Two sisters sought at eve my door;
Two song-birds wandering from their nest,
A gray old farmhouse in the West.

How fresh of life the younger one,
Half smiles, half tears, like rain in sun!
Her gravest mood could scarce displace
The dimples of her nut-brown face.

Wit sparkled on her lips not less
For quick and tremulous tenderness;

SEPTEMBER

And, following close her merriest glance,
Dreamed through her eyes the heart's romance.
THE SINGER.

5

Meyerbeer, 1791; Archbishop Trench, 1807.

FOR weeks the clouds had raked the hills
   And vexed the vales with raining,
And all the woods were sad with mist,
   And all the brooks complaining.

At last, a sudden night-storm tore
   The mountain veils asunder,
And swept the valleys clean before
   The besom of the thunder.

Clear drawn against the hard blue sky,
   The peaks had winter's keenness;
And, close on autumn's frost, the vales
   Had more than June's fresh greenness.

It was as if the summer's late
   Atoning for its sadness
Had borrowed every season's charm
   To end its days in gladness.
AMONG THE HILLS.

SEPTEMBER

6

Lafayette, 1757.

IF the stream had no quiet eddying place, could we so admire its cascade over the rocks? Were there no clouds, could we so hail the sky shining through them in its still calm purity?

THE BEAUTIFUL.

7

John Greenleaf Whittier died, 1892.

WHEN on my day of life the night is falling,
  And, in the winds from unsunned spaces blown,
I hear far voices out of darkness calling
  My feet to paths unknown,

Thou who hast made my home of life so pleasant,
  Leave not its tenant when its walls decay;
O Love Divine, O Helper ever present,
  Be Thou my strength and stay!

Be near me when all else is from me drifting;
  Earth, sky, home's pictures, days of shade and shine,
And kindly faces to my own uplifting
  The love which answers mine.

AT LAST.

SEPTEMBER

8

. Ariosto, 1474 ; A. W. Schlegel, 1767.

I HAVE but Thee, my Father! let Thy spirit
    Be with me then to comfort and uphold ;
No gate of pearl, no branch of palm I merit,
    Nor street of shining gold.

Suffice it if — my good and ill unreckoned,
    And both forgiven through Thy abounding grace —
I find myself by hands familiar beckoned
    Unto my fitting place.

Some humble door among Thy many mansions,
    Some sheltering shade where sin and striving cease,
And flows forever through heaven's green expansions
    The river of Thy peace.
                              AT LAST.

9

Thomas Hutchinson, 1711 ; J. H. Shorthouse, 1834.

I PRAY the prayer of Plato old :
    God make thee beautiful within,
And let thine eyes the good behold
    In everything save sin.

SEPTEMBER

Imagination held in check
  To serve, not rule, thy poisèd mind;
Thy Reason, at the frown or beck
  Of Conscience, loose or bind.
My Namesake.

10

Mungo Park, 1771; Philip Gilbert Hamerton, 1834.

Not alone in tones of awe and power
  He speaks to man;
The cloudy horror of the thunder-shower
  His rainbows span;
  And where the caravan
Winds o'er the desert, leaving, as in air
The crane-flock leaves, no trace of passage there,
  He gives the weary eye
The palm-leaf shadow for the hot noon hours,
  And on its branches dry
Calls out the acacia's flowers.
To Avis Keene.

11

James Thomson, 1700.

Nothing before, nothing behind;
  The steps of Faith
Fall on the seeming void, and find
  The rock beneath.

SEPTEMBER

The Present, the Present is all thou hast
    For thy sure possessing;
Like the patriarch's angel hold it fast
    Till it gives its blessing.
MY SOUL AND I.

12

Charles Dudley Warner, 1829.

FROM the clefts of mountain rocks,
    Through the dark of lowland firs,
Flash the eyes and flow the locks
    Of the mystic Vanishers!

And the fisher in his skiff,
    And the hunter on the moss,
Hear their call from cape and cliff,
    See their hands the birch-leaves toss.

Wistful, longing, through the green
    Twilight of the clustered pines,
In their faces rarely seen
    Beauty more than mortal shines.
THE VANISHERS.

13

James Shirley, 1596.

HERE, though unreached the goal we sought,
Its own reward our toil has brought:

SEPTEMBER

The winding water's sounding rush,
The long note of the hermit thrush,

The turquoise lakes, the glimpse of pond
And river track, and, vast, beyond
Broad meadows belted round with pines,
The grand uplift of mountain lines!

So failure wins; the consequence
Of loss becomes its recompense;
And evermore the end shall tell
The unreached ideal guided well.
THE SEEKING OF THE WATERFALL.

14

John Harvard died, 1638; Alexander von Humboldt, 1769.

You should have seen that long hill-range
　With gaps of brightness riven, —
How through each pass and hollow streamed
　The purpling lights of heaven, —

Rivers of gold-mist flowing down
　From far celestial fountains, —
The great sun flaming through the rifts
　Beyond the wall of mountains!
AMONG THE HILLS.

SEPTEMBER

15

James Fenimore Cooper, 1789; J. G. Percival, 1795.

LIFT we the twilight curtains of the Past,
   And, turning from familiar sight and sound,
Sadly and full of reverence let us cast
   A glance upon Tradition's shadowy ground,
Led by the few pale lights which, glimmering round
   That dim, strange land of Eld, seem dying fast;
And that which history gives not to the eye,
The faded coloring of Time's tapestry,
Let Fancy with her dream-dipped brush supply.
              THE BRIDAL OF PENNACOOK.

16

Samuel Adams, 1722; Francis Parkman, 1823.

O PAINTER of the fruits and flowers,
   We own Thy wise design,
Whereby these human hands of ours
   May share the work of Thine!

Apart from Thee we plant in vain
   The root and sow the seed;
Thy early and Thy later rain,
   Thy sun and dew we need.

Our toil is sweet with thankfulness,
   Our burden is our boon;
The curse of Earth's gray morning is
   The blessing of its noon.
              GARDEN.

SEPTEMBER

17

Samuel Hopkins, 1721.

HONOR to the true man ever, who takes his life in his hands, and, at all hazards, speaks the word which is given him to utter, whether men will hear or forbear, whether the end thereof is to be praise or censure, gratitude or hatred. It well may be doubted whether on that Sabbath day the angels of God, in their wide survey of His universe, looked upon a nobler spectacle than that of the minister of Newport, rising up before his slave-holding congregation, and demanding, in the name of the Highest, the " deliverance of the captive, and the opening of prison doors to them that were bound."
SAMUEL HOPKINS.

18

Samuel Johnson, 1709; Joseph Story, 1779.

FAREWELL! these smiling hills must wear
    Too soon their wintry frown,
And snow-cold winds from off them shake
    The maple's red leaves down.
But I shall see a summer sun
    Still setting broad and low;
The mountain slopes shall blush and bloom,
    The golden water flow.
A lover's claim is mine on all
    I see to have and hold, —

SEPTEMBER

The rose-light of perpetual hills,
And sunsets never cold!
SUNSET ON THE BEARCAMP.

19

Hartley Coleridge, 1796.

HAS life's infancy only been provided for, and beyond this poor nursery-chamber of Time is there no play-ground for the soul's youth, no broad fields for its manhood?
SCOTTISH REFORMERS.

20

THE river wound as it should wind;
 Their place the mountains took;
The white torn fringes of their clouds
 Wore no unwonted look.

Yet ne'er before that river's rim
 Was pressed by feet of mine,
Never before mine eyes had crossed
 That broken mountain line.

A presence, strange at once and known,
 Walked with me as my guide;
The skirts of some forgotten life
 Trailed noiseless at my side.

SEPTEMBER

Was it a dim-remembered dream?
Or glimpse through æons old?
The secret which the mountains kept
The river never told.
                                A MYSTERY.

21

St. Matthew; Savonarola, 1452.

SUFFICE it now. — In time to be
Shall holier altars rise to Thee, —
Thy Church our broad humanity!

White flowers of love its walls shall climb,
Soft bells of peace shall ring its chime,
Its days shall all be holy time.

A sweeter song shall then be heard, —
The music of the world's accord
Confessing Christ, the Inward Word!

That song shall swell from shore to shore,
One hope, one faith, one love, restore
The seamless robe that Jesus wore.
                                HYMN.

22

Michael Faraday, 1791; Dr. John Brown, 1810.

WE need love's tender lessons taught
    As only weakness can;
God hath His small interpreters;
    The child must teach the man.

SEPTEMBER

We wander wide through evil years,
 Our eyes of faith grow dim;
But he is freshest from His hands
 And nearest unto Him!
                    CHILD-SONGS.

23

Jane Taylor, 1783; Karl Theodor Körner, 1791.

MORE than clouds of purple trail
 In the gold of setting day;
More than gleams of wing or sail
 Beckon from the sea-mist gray.

Glimpses of immortal youth,
 Gleams and glories seen and flown,
Far-heard voices sweet with truth,
 Airs from viewless Eden blown, —

Beauty that eludes our grasp,
 Sweetness that transcends our taste,
Loving hands we may not clasp,
 Shining feet that mock our haste.
                    THE VANISHERS.

24

John Marshall, 1755.

HOPE not the cure of sin till Self is dead;
Forget it in love's service, and the debt
Thou canst not pay the angels shall forget;

SEPTEMBER

Heaven's gate is shut to him who comes alone;
Save thou a soul, and it shall save thy own!
THE TWO RABBINS.

25

Felicia Dorothea Hemans, 1794.

WHEN did Age transfer to Youth
The hard-gained lessons of its day?
Each lip must learn the taste of truth,
Each foot must feel its way.

We cannot hold the hands of choice
That touch or shun life's fateful keys;
The whisper of the inward voice
Is more than homilies.
A NAME.

26

Lord Collingwood, 1750.

LET winds that blow from heaven refresh,
Dear Lord, the languid air;
And let the weakness of the flesh
Thy strength of spirit share.

And, if the eye must fail of light,
The ear forget to hear,
Make clearer still the spirit's sight,
More fine the inward ear!

SEPTEMBER

Be near me in mine hours of need
To soothe, or cheer, or warn,
And down these slopes of sunset lead
As up the hills of morn !
My Birthday.

27

Bossuet, 1627.

IT becomes all to hope and labor for the coming of that day when the hymns of Cowper and the Confessions of Augustine, the humane philosophy of Channing and the devout meditations of Thomas à Kempis, the simple essays of Woolman and the glowing periods of Bossuet, shall be regarded as the offspring of one spirit and one faith, — lights of a common altar, and precious stones in the temple of the one universal Church.
Pope Night.

28

Francis Turner Palgrave, 1824.

For there was freedom in that wakening time
Of tender souls; to differ was not crime;
The varying bells made up the perfect chime.

On lips unlike was laid the altar's coal,
The white, clear light, tradition-colored, stole
Through the stained oriel of each human soul.
The Pennsylvania Pilgrim.

SEPTEMBER

29

Michaelmas; William, Lord Russell, 1639; Lady Russell
died, 1723.

I FAIN would thank Thee that my mortal life
  Has reached the hour (albeit through care and
    pain)
When Good and Evil, as for final strife,
  Close dim and vast on Armageddon's plain ;
And Michael and his angels once again
  Drive howling back the Spirits of the Night.
Oh for the faith to read the signs aright
And, from the angle of Thy perfect sight,
  See Truth's white banner floating on before ;
  And the Good Cause, despite of venal friends,
  And base expedients, move to noble ends ;
  See Peace with Freedom make to Time amends,
And, through its cloud of dust, the threshing-floor,
  Flailed by the thunder, heaped with chaffless
    grain!
1856.   WHAT OF THE DAY?

30

    FOR pearls that gem
    A diadem
The diver in the deep sea dies ;
    The regal right
    We boast to-night
Is ours through costlier sacrifice ;

SEPTEMBER

The blood of Vane,
His prison pain
Who traced the path the Pilgrim trod,
And hers whose faith
Drew strength from death,
And prayed her Russell up to God!

The shadow rend,
And o'er us bend,
O martyrs, with your crowns and palms;
Breathe through these throngs
Your battle songs,
Your scaffold prayers, and dungeon psalms!
. . . .
To party claims
And private aims,
Reveal that august face of Truth,
Whereto are given
The age of heaven,
The beauty of immortal youth.

THE EVE OF ELECTION.

October

FOR AN AUTUMN FESTIVAL

ONCE more the liberal year laughs out
 O'er richer stores than gems or gold;
Once more with harvest-song and shout
 Is Nature's bloodless triumph told.

Our common mother rests and sings,
 Like Ruth, among her garnered sheaves;
Her lap is full of goodly things,
 Her brow is bright with autumn leaves.

Oh, favors every year made new!
 Oh, gifts with rain and sunshine sent!
The bounty overruns our due,
 The fulness shames our discontent.

We shut our eyes, the flowers bloom on;
 We murmur, but the corn-ears fill,
We choose the shadow, but the sun
 That casts it shines behind us still.

God gives us with our rugged soil
 The power to make it Eden-fair,
And richer fruits to crown our toil
 Than summer-wedded islands bear.

OCTOBER

Who murmurs at his lot to-day?
  Who scorns his native fruit and bloom?
Or sighs for dainties far away,
  Beside the bounteous board of home?

Thank Heaven, instead, that Freedom's arm
  Can change a rocky soil to gold,—
That brave and generous lives can warm
  A clime with northern ices cold.

And let these altars, wreathed with flowers
  And piled with fruits, awake again
Thanksgivings for the golden hours,
  The early and the latter rain!

OCTOBER

1

Rufus Choate, 1799.

THE airs of spring may never play
    Among the ripening corn,
Nor freshness of the flowers of May
    Blow through the autumn morn;

Yet shall the blue-eyed gentian look
    Through fringëd lids to heaven,
And the pale aster in the brook
    Shall see its image given;—

The woods shall wear their robes of praise,
    The south-wind softly sigh,
And sweet, calm days in golden haze
    Melt down the amber sky.
                  MY PSALM.

2

W. E. Channing died, 1842.

NOT vainly did old poets tell,
    Nor vainly did old genius paint
God's great and crowning miracle, —
    The hero and the saint!

For even in a faithless day
    Can we our sainted ones discern;
And feel, while with them on the way,
    Our hearts within us burn.

OCTOBER

In vain shall Rome her portals bar,
    And shut from him her saintly prize,
Whom, in the world's great calendar,
    All men shall canonize.
CHANNING.

3

George Bancroft, 1800; George Ripley, 1802.

ALL which is real now remaineth,
    And fadeth never:
The hand which upholds it now sustaineth
    The soul forever.

And that cloud itself, which now before thee
    Lies dark in view,
Shall with beams of light from the inner glory
    Be stricken through.

And like meadow mist through autumn's dawn
    Uprolling thin,
Its thickest folds when about thee drawn
    Let sunlight in.
MY SOUL AND I.

4

Guizot, 1787; J. F. Millet, 1814.

BEAUTIFUL yet for me this autumn day
Melts on its sunset hills; and, far away,

OCTOBER

For me the Ocean lifts its solemn psalm,
To me the pine-woods whisper; and for me
Yon river, winding through its vales of calm,
By greenest banks, with asters purple-starred,
And gentian bloom and golden-rod made gay,
Flows down in silent gladness to the sea,
Like a pure spirit to its great reward!
THE PRISONERS OF NAPLES.

5

Jonathan Edwards, 1703.

IN the church of the wilderness Edwards wrought,
Shaping his creed at the forge of thought;
And with Thor's own hammer welded and bent
The iron links of his argument,
Which strove to grasp in its mighty span
The purpose of God and the fate of man!
Yet faithful still, in his daily round
To the weak, and the poor, and sin-sick found,
The schoolman's lore and the casuist's art
Drew warmth and life from his fervent heart.
Had he not seen in the solitudes
Of his deep and dark Northampton woods
A vision of love about him fall?
Not the blinding splendor which fell on Saul,
But the tenderer glory that rests on them
Who walk in the New Jerusalem,
Where never the sun nor moon are known,
But the Lord and His love are the light alone!
THE PREACHER.

OCTOBER

6

Jenny Lind, 1821.

WHO hates, hates Thee, who loves becomes
    Therein to Thee allied;
All sweet accords of hearts and homes
    In Thee are multiplied.

Deep strike Thy roots, O heavenly Vine,
    Within our earthly sod,
Most human and yet most divine,
    The flower of man and God!
OUR MASTER.

7

Robert Dinsmore, 1757.

A GENIAL, jovial, large-hearted old man, simple as a child, and betraying, neither in look nor manner, that he was accustomed to

> "Feed on thoughts which voluntary move
> Harmonious numbers."

Peace to him! . . . In the ancient burial-ground of Windham, by the side of his "beloved Molly," and in view of the old meeting-house, there is a mound of earth, where, every spring, green grasses tremble in the wind, and the warm sunshine calls out the flowers. There, gathered like one of his own ripe sheaves, the farmer poet sleeps with his fathers.
ROBERT DINSMORE.

OCTOBER

8

E. C. Stedman, 1833; John Hay, 1839.

POET and friend of poets, if thy glass
Detects no flower in winter's tuft of grass,
Let this slight token of the debt I owe
  Outlive for thee December's frozen day,
And, like the arbutus budding under snow,
Take bloom and fragrance from some morn of
    May
When he who gives it shall have gone the way
Where faith shall see and reverent trust shall
    know.
To E. C. S.
[Dedication to At Sundown.]

9

Cervantes, 1549; Giuseppe Verdi, 1813.

WE dropped the seed o'er hill and plain,
  Beneath the sun of May,
And frightened from our sprouting grain
  The robber crows away.

All through the long, bright days of June
  Its leaves grew green and fair,
And waved in hot midsummer's noon
  Its soft and yellow hair.

And now, with autumn's moonlit eves,
  Its harvest-time has come,

OCTOBER

We pluck away the frosted leaves,
And bear the treasure home.
THE CORN-SONG.

10

Benjamin West, 1738; Hugh Miller, 1802.

AUTUMN'S earliest frost had given
   To the woods below
Hues of beauty, such as heaven
   Lendeth to its bow;
And the soft breeze from the west
Scarcely broke their dreamy rest.
THE FOUNTAIN.

11

NOWHERE fairer, sweeter, rarer,
Does the golden-locked fruit bearer
   Through his painted woodlands stray,
Than where hillside oaks and beeches
Overlook the long, blue reaches,
Silver coves and pebbled beaches,
   And green isles of Casco Bay;
   Nowhere day, for delay,
With a tenderer look beseeches,
"Let me with my charmed earth stay."
THE RANGER.

OCTOBER

12

On all his sad or restless moods
　The patient peace of Nature stole;
The quiet of the fields and woods
　Sank deep into his soul.

He worshipped as his fathers did,
　And kept the faith of childish days,
And, howsoe'er he strayed or slid,
　He loved the good old ways.

The simple tastes, the kindly traits,
　The tranquil air, and gentle speech,
The silence of the soul that waits
　For more than man to teach.
　　　　　　　　　　My Namesake.

13

Elizabeth Fry died, 1845.

The Gospel of a life like hers
　Is more than books or scrolls.
From scheme and creed the light goes out,
　The saintly fact survives;
The blessed Master none can doubt
　Revealed in holy lives.
　　　　　　　　　The Friend's Burial.

OCTOBER

14
William Penn, 1644.

GATHERED from many sects, the Quaker brought
His old beliefs, adjusting to the thought
That moved his soul the creed his fathers taught:

One faith alone, so broad that all mankind
Within themselves its secret witness find,
The soul's communion with the Eternal mind.

The Spirit's law, the Inward Rule and Guide,
Scholar and peasant, lord and serf, allied,
The polished Penn and Cromwell's Ironside.
THE PENNSYLVANIA PILGRIM.

15
Allan Ramsay, 1686; Wilhelm von Kaulbach, 1805.

THE summer grains were harvested; the stubble-
    fields lay dry,
Where June winds rolled, in light and shade, the
    pale green waves of rye;
But still, on gentle hill-slopes, in valleys fringed
    with wood,
Ungathered, bleaching in the sun, the heavy corn
    crop stood.

Bent low, by autumn's wind and rain, through husks
    that, dry and sere,
Unfolded from their ripened charge, shone out the
    yellow ear;

OCTOBER

Beneath, the turnip lay concealed, in many a verdant fold,
And glistened in the slanting light the pumpkin's sphere of gold.
THE HUSKERS.

16

Noah Webster, 1758; Robert Stephenson, 1803.

OH, fruit loved of boyhood! the old days recalling,
When wood-grapes were purpling and brown nuts were falling!
When wild, ugly faces we carved in its skin,
Glaring out through the dark with a candle within!
When we laughed round the corn-heap, with hearts all in tune,
Our chair a broad pumpkin, — our lantern the moon,
Telling tales of the fairy who travelled like steam,
In a pumpkin-shell coach, with two rats for her team!
THE PUMPKIN.

17

Sir John Bowring, 1792.

WITH silence only as their benediction,
    God's angels come
Where, in the shadow of a great affliction,
    The soul sits dumb!

OCTOBER

Yet, would I say what thy own heart approveth:
  Our Father's will,
Calling to Him the dear one whom He loveth,
  Is mercy still.

God calls our loved ones, but we lose not wholly
  What He hath given;
They live on earth, in thought and deed, as truly
  As in His heaven.
            To My Friend on the Death of His Sister.

18

St. Luke; Henry Taylor, 1800.

For lo! in human hearts unseen
  The Healer dwelleth still,
And they who make His temples clean
  The best subserve His will.

The holiest task by Heaven decreed,
  An errand all divine,
The burden of our common need
  To render less is thine.
                    The Healer.

19

John Adams, 1735; Leigh Hunt, 1784.

It was the pleasant harvest-time,
  When cellar-bins are closely stowed,
  And garrets bend beneath their load,

OCTOBER

And the old swallow-haunted barns, —
Brown-gabled, long, and full of seams
Through which the moted sunlight streams,

And winds blow freshly in, to shake
The red plumes of the roosted cocks,
And the loose hay-mow's scented locks, —

Are filled with summer's ripened stores,
Its odorous grass and barley sheaves,
From their low scaffolds to their eaves.
MABEL MARTIN.

20

Sir Christopher Wren, 1632; Thomas Hughes, 1823.

As long as a wandering pigeon shall search
The fields below from his white-oak perch,
When the barley-harvest is ripe and shorn,
And the dry husks fall from the standing corn;
As long as Nature shall not grow old,
Nor drop her work from her doting hold,
And her care for the Indian corn forget,
And the yellow rows in pairs to set; —
So long shall Christians here be born,
Grow up and ripen as God's sweet corn! —
By the beak of bird, by the breath of frost,
Shall never a holy ear be lost,
But, husked by Death in the Planter's sight,
Be sown again in the fields of light!
THE PROPHECY OF SAMUEL SEWALL.

OCTOBER

21

S. T. Coleridge, 1772; Alphonse de Lamartine, 1790.

IT was late in mild October, and the long autumnal rain
Had left the summer harvest-fields all green with grass again;
The first sharp frosts had fallen, leaving all the woodlands gay
With the hues of summer's rainbow, or the meadow-flowers of May.

Through a thin, dry mist, that morning, the sun rose broad and red,
At first a rayless disk of fire, he brightened as he sped;
Yet, even his noontide glory fell chastened and subdued,
On the cornfields and the orchards, and softly pictured wood.
THE HUSKERS.

22

Franz Liszt, 1811.

AND all that quiet afternoon, slow sloping to the night,
He wove with golden shuttle the haze with yellow light;

OCTOBER

Slanting through the painted beeches, he glorified
    the hill;
And, beneath it, pond and meadow lay brighter,
    greener still.

From spire and barn looked westerly the patient
    weathercocks;
But even the birches on the hill stood motionless
    as rocks.
No sound was in the woodlands, save the squirrel's
    dropping shell,
And the yellow leaves among the boughs, low rustling as they fell.
                                    THE HUSKERS.

23

Francis Jeffrey, 1773.

WITH mingled sound of horns and bells,
    A far-heard clang, the wild geese fly,
Storm-sent, from Arctic moors and fells,
    Like a great arrow through the sky,
Two dusky lines converged in one,
Chasing the southward-flying sun;
While the brave snow-bird and the hardy jay
Call to them from the pines, as if to bid them stay.
                    THE LAST WALK IN AUTUMN.

OCTOBER

24

Daniel Webster died, 1852.

AH, cruel fate, that closed to thee,
O sleeper by the Northern sea,
The gates of opportunity !
God fills the gaps of human need,
Each crisis brings its word and deed.
Wise men and strong we did not lack;
But still, with memory turning back,
In the dark hours we thought of thee,
And thy lone grave beside the sea.
. . . .
But, where thy native mountains bare
Their foreheads to diviner air,
Fit emblem of enduring fame,
One lofty summit keeps thy name.
And evermore that mountain mass
Seems climbing from the shadowy pass
To light, as if to manifest
Thy nobler self, thy life at best !
THE LOST OCCASION.

25

Lord Macaulay, 1800.

HE who lies where the minster's groined arches
    curve down
To the tomb-crowded transept of England's renown,

OCTOBER

The glorious essayist, by genius enthroned,
Whose pen as a sceptre the Muses all owned, —

How vainly he labored to sully with blame
The white bust of Penn, in the niche of his fame! . . .
For the sake of his gifts, and the works that outlive him,
And his brave words for freedom, we freely forgive him!
THE QUAKER ALUMNI.

26

Count von Moltke, 1800.

SEARCH thine own heart. What paineth thee
In others in thyself may be;
All dust is frail, all flesh is weak;
Be thou the true man thou dost seek!
THE CHAPEL OF THE HERMITS.

27

THE blessing of her quiet life
  Fell on us like the dew;
And good thoughts where her footsteps pressed
  Like fairy blossoms grew.

Sweet promptings unto kindest deeds
  Were in her very look;
We read her face, as one who reads
  A true and holy book:

OCTOBER

The measure of a blessed hymn,
  To which our hearts could move;
The breathing of an inward psalm,
  A canticle of love.
                        GONE.

28

Erasmus, 1467.

FRINGED with gold their mantles flow
  On the slopes of westering knolls;
In the wind they whisper low
  Of the Sunset Land of Souls.

Doubt who may, O friend of mine!
  Thou and I have seen them too;
On before with beck and sign
  Still they glide, and we pursue. . . .

Gentle eyes we closed below,
  Tender voices heard once more,
Smile and call us, as they go
  On and onward, still before.
                        THE VANISHERS.

29

John Keats, 1795.

GOD'S angels come not as of old
  The Syrian shepherds knew them;
In reddening dawns, in sunset gold,
  And warm noon lights I view them.

OCTOBER

Nor need there is, in times like this
  When heaven to earth draws nearer,
Of wing or song as witnesses
  To make their presence clearer.

O stream of life, whose swifter flow
  Is of the end forewarning,
Methinks thy sundown afterglow
  Seems less of night than morning!
St. Martin's Summer.

30

Enough that blessings undeserved
  Have marked my erring track; —
That whereso'er my feet have swerved,
  His chastening turned me back; —

That more and more a Providence
  Of love is understood,
Making the springs of time and sense
  Sweet with eternal good; —

That death seems but a covered way
  Which opens into light,
Wherein no blinded child can stray
  Beyond the Father's sight.
My Psalm.

OCTOBER

31

<small>All Hallows Eve; John Evelyn, 1620.</small>

IF it be true that, according to Cornelius Agrippa, "a wood fire doth drive away dark spirits," it is, nevertheless, also true that around it the simple superstitions of our ancestors still love to linger; and there the half-sportful, half-serious charms of which I have spoken are oftenest resorted to.

. . . .

Within the circle of the light of the open fire safely might the young conjurers question destiny; for none but kindly and gentle messengers from Wonderland could venture among them. And who of us, looking back to those long autumnal evenings of childhood when the glow of the kitchen-fire rested on the beloved faces of home, does not feel that there is truth and beauty in what the quaint old author just quoted affirms? "As the spirits of darkness grow stronger in the dark, so good spirits, which are angels of light, are multiplied and strengthened, not only by the divine light of the sun and stars, but also by the light of our common woodfires."

CHARMS AND FAIRY FAITH.

November

A DAY

TALK not of sad November, when a day
   Of warm, glad sunshine fills the sky of noon,
   And a wind, borrowed from some morn of June,
Stirs the brown grasses and the leafless spray.

On the unfrosted pool the pillared pines
   Lay their long shafts of shadow: the small rill,
   Singing a pleasant song of summer still,
A line of silver, down the hill-slope shines.

Hushed the bird-voices and the hum of bees,
   In the thin grass the crickets pipe no more;
   But still the squirrel hoards his winter store,
And drops his nutshells from the shag-bark trees.

Softly the dark green hemlocks whisper: high
   Above, the spires of yellowing larches show,
   Where the woodpecker and home-loving crow
And jay and nut-hatch winter's threat defy.

O gracious beauty, ever new and old!
   O sights and sounds of nature, doubly dear
   When the low sunshine warns the closing year
Of snow-blown fields and waves of Arctic cold!

NOVEMBER

Close to my heart I fold each lovely thing
 The sweet day yields; and, not disconsolate,
 With the calm patience of the woods I wait
For leaf and blossom when God gives us Spring!

NOVEMBER

1

All Saints; Antonio Canova, 1757.

WHERE now with pain thou treadest, trod
The whitest of the saints of God!
To show thee where their feet were set,
The light which led them shineth yet.

The footprints of the life divine,
Which marked their path, remain in thine;
And that great Life, transfused in theirs,
Awaits thy faith, thy love, thy prayers!
THE CHAPEL OF THE HERMITS.

2

Marie Antoinette, 1755.

SOON or late to all our dwellings come the spectres of the mind,
Doubts and fears and dread forebodings, in the darkness undefined;
Round us throng the grim projections of the heart and of the brain,
And our pride of strength is weakness, and the cunning hand is vain.

In the dark we cry like children; and no answer from on high
Breaks the crystal spheres of silence, and no white wings downward fly;

NOVEMBER

But the heavenly help we pray for comes to faith,
    and not to sight,
And our prayers themselves drive backward all the
    spirits of the night!
THE GARRISON OF CAPE ANN.

3

William Cullen Bryant, 1794.

WE praise not now the poet's art,
    The rounded beauty of his song;
Who weighs him from his life apart
    Must do his nobler nature wrong.

Not for the eye, familiar grown
    With charms to common sight denied, —
The marvellous gift he shares alone
    With him who walked on Rydal-side.

Not for rapt hymn nor woodland lay,
    Too grave for smiles, too sweet for tears;
We speak his praise who wears to-day
    The glory of his seventy years.
1864.   BRYANT ON HIS BIRTHDAY.

4

James Montgomery, 1771.

THE grass is browning on the hills;
    No pale, belated flowers recall
The astral fringes of the rills,

NOVEMBER

And drearily the dead vines fall,
Frost-blackened, from the roadside wall.

Yet through the gray and sombre wood,
  Against the dusk of fir and pine,
Last of their floral sisterhood,
  The hazel's yellow blossoms shine,
  The tawny gold of Afric's mine !
                        HAZEL-BLOSSOMS.

5

Washington Allston, 1779.

ALONG the river's summer walk,
  The withered tufts of asters nod;
And trembles on its arid stalk
  The hoar plume of the golden-rod.
And on a ground of sombre fir,
And azure-studded juniper,
The silver birch its buds of purple shows,
And scarlet berries tell where bloomed the sweet
    wild-rose !
                    THE LAST WALK IN AUTUMN.

6

C. C. Felton, 1807; Richard Jefferies, 1848.

OUR hearts grow cold,
  We lightly hold
A right which brave men died to gain;

NOVEMBER

The stake, the cord,
The axe, the sword,
Grim nurses at its birth of pain.

Look from the sky,
Like God's great eye,
Thou solemn moon, with searching beam,
   Till in the sight
   Of thy pure light
Our mean self-seekings meaner seem.
                    THE EVE OF ELECTION.

7

THAT care and trial seem at last,
   Through Memory's sunset air,
Like mountain-ranges overpast,
   In purple distance fair; —

That all the jarring notes of life
   Seem blending in a psalm,
And all the angles of its strife
   Slow rounding into calm.

And so the shadows fall apart,
   And so the west-winds play;
And all the windows of my heart
   I open to the day.
                    MY PSALM.

NOVEMBER

8

Robert, Earl Lytton, 1831.

THE summer and the winter here
  Midway a truce are holding,
A soft, consenting atmosphere
  Their tents of peace enfolding.

The silent woods, the lonely hills,
  Rise solemn in their gladness;
The quiet that the valley fills
  Is scarcely joy or sadness.
                    ST. MARTIN'S SUMMER.

9

MY autumn time and Nature's hold
  A dreamy tryst together,
And, both grown old, about us fold
  The golden-tissued weather.

I lean my heart against the day
  To feel its bland caressing;
I will not let it pass away
  Before it leaves its blessing.
                    ST. MARTIN'S SUMMER.

NOVEMBER

10

Luther, 1483; Goldsmith, 1728; Schiller, 1759; S. G. Howe, 1801.

SMILE not, fair unbeliever!
  One man, at least, I know,
Who might wear the crest of Bayard
  Or Sidney's plume of snow.

True as the knights of story,
  Sir Lancelot and his peers,
Brave in his calm endurance
  As they in tilt of spears.

Wouldst know him now? Behold him,
  The Cadmus of the blind,
Giving the dumb lip language,
  The idiot clay a mind.
              THE HERO.

11

Martinmas; T. B. Aldrich, 1836.

THOUGH flowers have perished at the touch
  Of Frost, the early comer,
I hail the season loved so much,
  The good St. Martin's summer.

O gracious morn, with rose-red dawn,
  And thin moon curving o'er it!
The old year's darling, latest born,
  More loved than all before it!

NOVEMBER

The sweet day, opening as a flower
Unfolds its petals tender,
Renews for us at noontide's hour
The summer's tempered splendor.
ST. MARTIN'S SUMMER.

12

Richard Baxter, 1615.

THE " Call to the Unconverted " and the " Saints' Everlasting Rest " belong to no time or sect. They speak the universal language of the wants and desires of the human soul. They take hold of the awful verities of life and death, righteousness and judgment to come. Through them the suffering and hunted minister of Kidderminster has spoken in warning, entreaty, and rebuke, or in tones of tenderest love and pity, to the hearts of the generations which have succeeded him.
RICHARD BAXTER.

13

St. Augustine, 354; Tegner, 1782; Edwin Booth, 1833.

THE fourteen centuries fall away
Between us and the Afric saint,
And at his side we urge, to-day,
The immemorial quest and old complaint.

No outward sign to us is given, —
From sea or earth comes no reply;
Hushed as the warm Numidian heaven
He vainly questioned, bends our frozen sky.

NOVEMBER

No victory comes of all our strife, —
From all we grasp the meaning slips;
The Sphinx sits at the gate of life,
With the old question on her awful lips.
THE SHADOW AND THE LIGHT.

14

L. J. M. Daguerre, 1787; Sir Charles Lyell, 1797.

I HAVE no answer for myself or thee,
Save that I learned beside my mother's knee;
"All is of God that is, and is to be;
And God is good." Let this suffice us still,
Resting in childlike trust upon His will
Who moves to His great ends unthwarted by the ill.
TRUST.

15

William Cowper, 1731; R. H. Dana, 1787.

AND if the tender ear be jarred
  That, haply, hears by turns
The saintly harp of Olney's bard,
  The pastoral pipe of Burns,
No discord mars His perfect plan
  Who gave them both a tongue;
For he who sings the love of man
  The love of God hath sung!
BURNS FESTIVAL.

NOVEMBER

16

John Bright, 1811; Charles Eliot Norton, 1827.

PRESS on! — the triumph shall be won
Of common rights and equal laws,
The glorious dream of Harrington,
And Sidney's good old cause:

Blessing the cotter and the crown,
　Sweetening worn Labor's bitter cup;
And, plucking not the highest down,
　Lifting the lowest up.
　　　　　　To the Reformers of England.

17

Sir Charles Eastlake, 1793; George Grote, 1794.

THE dear Christ dwells not afar,
The king of some remoter star,
Listening, at times, with flattered ear
To homage wrung from selfish fear,
But here, amidst the poor and blind,
The bound and suffering of our kind,
In works we do, in prayers we pray,
Life of our life, He lives to-day.
　　　　　　The Meeting.

NOVEMBER

18

David Wilkie, 1785; Asa Gray, 1810.

O'ER the bare woods, whose outstretched hands
Plead with the leaden heavens in vain,
I see, beyond the valley lands,
The sea's long level dim with rain.
Around me all things, stark and dumb,
Seem praying for the snows to come,
And, for the summer bloom and greenness gone,
With winter's sunset lights and dazzling morn
atone.
THE LAST WALK IN AUTUMN.

19

Elisha Mulford, 1833.

UNNOTED as the setting of a star
He passed; and sect and party scarcely knew
When from their midst a sage and seer withdrew
To fitter audience, where the great dead are
In God's republic of the heart and mind,
Leaving no purer, nobler soul behind.
MULFORD.

20

Thomas Chatterton, 1752; Queen Margherita, 1851.

FOREVER round the Mercy-seat
The guiding lights of Love shall burn;

NOVEMBER

But what if, habit-bound, thy feet
Shall lack the will to turn?

What if thine eye refuse to see,
 Thine ear of Heaven's free welcome fail,
And thou a willing captive be,
 Thyself thy own dark jail?

Oh, doom beyond the saddest guess,
 As the long years of God unroll,
To make thy dreary selfishness
 The prison of a soul!
                             THE ANSWER.

21

Bryan Waller Procter, 1787.

NEVER yet in darkest mood
Doubted I that Thou wast good,
Nor mistook my will for fate,
Pain of sin for heavenly hate, —
Never dreamed the gates of pearl
Rise from out the burning marl,
Or that good can only live
Of the bad conservative,
And through counterpoise of hell
Heaven alone be possible.
            ANDREW RYKMAN'S PRAYER.

NOVEMBER

22

"George Eliot," 1819.

BEFORE the Ender comes, whose charioteer
Is swift or slow Disease, lay up each year
Thy harvests of well-doing, wealth that kings
Nor thieves can take away. When all the things
Thou callest thine, goods, pleasures, honors fall,
Thou in thy virtue shalt survive them all.
LAYING UP TREASURE.

23

FAIRER hands never wrought at a pastry more fine,
Brighter eyes never watched o'er its baking, than
  thine!
And the prayer, which my mouth is too full to express,
Swells my heart that thy shadow may never be less,
That the days of thy lot may be lengthened below,
And the fame of thy worth like a pumpkin-vine
  grow,
And thy life be as sweet, and its last sunset sky
Golden-tinted and fair as thy own Pumpkin pie!
THE PUMPKIN.

24

Laurence Sterne, 1713; H. T. Buckle, 1821.

THE horn, on Sabbath morning, through the still
  and frosty air,
From Spurwink, Pool, and Black Point, called to
  sermon and to prayer,

NOVEMBER

To the goodly house of worship, where, in order
    due and fit,
As by public vote directed, classed and ranked the
    people sit;

Mistress first and goodwife after, clerkly squire
    before the clown,
From the brave coat, lace-embroidered, to the gray
    frock, shading down.
MARY GARVIN.

25

THE wise old Doctor went his round,
Just pausing at our door to say,
In the brief autocratic way
Of one who, prompt at Duty's call,
Was free to urge her claim on all,
    That some poor neighbor sick abed
At night our mother's aid would need.
For, one in generous thought and deed,
    What mattered in the sufferer's sight
    The Quaker matron's inward light,
The Doctor's mail of Calvin's creed?
All hearts confess the saints elect
    Who, twain in faith, in love agree,
And melt not in an acid sect
    The Christian pearl of charity!
SNOW-BOUND.

NOVEMBER

26

Empress Marie Féodorovna, 1847.

AH! on Thanksgiving day, when from East and
  from West,
From North and from South come the pilgrim and
  guest,
When the gray-haired New-Englander sees round
  his board
The old broken links of affection restored,
When the care-wearied man seeks his mother once
  more,
And the worn matron smiles where the girl smiled
  before.
THE PUMPKIN.

27

Frances Anne Kemble, 1809.

STILL on the lips of all we question
  The finger of God's silence lies ;
Will the lost hands in ours be folded ?
  Will the shut eyelids ever rise ?

O friend ! no proof beyond this yearning,
  This outreach of our hearts, we need ;
God will not mock the hope He giveth,
  No love He prompts shall vainly plead.

No dreary splendors wait our coming
  Where rapt ghost sits from ghost apart ;

NOVEMBER

Homeward we go to Heaven's thanksgiving,
The harvest-gathering of the heart.
To Lydia Maria Child.

28

William Blake, 1757.

O Christ of God! whose life and death
  Our own have reconciled,
Most quietly, most tenderly
  Take home Thy star-named child!

Thy grace is in her patient eyes,
  Thy words are on her tongue;
The very silence round her seems
  As if the angels sung.

Her smile is as a listening child's
  Who hears its mother call;
The lilies of Thy perfect peace
  About her pillow fall.

Oh, less for her than for ourselves
  We bow our heads and pray;
Her setting star, like Bethlehem's,
  To Thee shall point the way!
Vesta

NOVEMBER

29

Sir Philip Sidney, 1554

BETTER to use the bit, than throw
The reins all loose on fancy's neck.
The liberal range of Art should be
The breadth of Christian liberty,
Restrained alone by challenge and alarm
Where its charmed footsteps tread the border
    land of harm.
                                THE TENT ON THE BEACH.

30

St. Andrew; Jonathan Swift, 1667; Theodor Mommsen, 1817.

LET the lowliest task be mine,
Grateful, so the work be Thine;
Let me find the humblest place
In the shadow of Thy grace:
Blest to me were any spot
Where temptation whispers not.
If there be some weaker one,
Give me strength to help him on;
If a blinder soul there be,
Let me guide him nearer Thee.
Make my mortal dreams come true
With the work I fain would do;
Clothe with life the weak intent,
Let me be the thing I meant.
                        ANDREW RYKMAN'S PRAYER.

December

A CHRISTMAS CARMEN

I

SOUND over all waters, reach out from all lands,
The chorus of voices, the clasping of hands;
Sing hymns that were sung by the stars of the morn,
Sing songs of the angels when Jesus was born!
　With glad jubilations
　Bring hope to the nations!
The dark night is ending and dawn has begun:
Rise, hope of the ages, arise like the sun,
　All speech flow to music, all hearts beat as one!

II

Sing the bridal of nations! with chorals of love
Sing out the war-vulture and sing in the dove,
Till the hearts of the peoples keep time in accord,
And the voice of the world is the voice of the Lord!
　Clasp hands of the nations
　In strong gratulations:
The dark night is ending and dawn has begun;
Rise, hope of the ages, arise like the sun,
　All speech flow to music, all hearts beat as one!

DECEMBER

III

Blow, bugles of battle, the marches of peace;
East, west, north, and south let the long quarrel
    cease:
Sing the song of great joy that the angels began,
Sing of glory to God and of good-will to man!
    Hark! joining in chorus
    The heavens bend o'er us!
The dark night is ending and dawn has begun;
Rise, hope of the ages, arise like the sun,
    All speech flow to music, all hearts beat as one!

DECEMBER

1

Alexandra, Princess of Wales, 1844.

THE sun that brief December day
Rose cheerless over hills of gray,
And, darkly circled, gave at noon
A sadder light than waning moon.
Slow tracing down the thickening sky
Its mute and ominous prophecy,
A portent seeming less than threat,
It sank from sight before it set.
A hard, dull bitterness of cold,
That checked, mid-vein, the circling race
Of life-blood in the sharpened face,
The coming of the snow-storm told.
The wind blew east; we heard the roar
Of Ocean on his wintry shore,
And felt the strong pulse throbbing there
Beat with low rhythm our inland air.
SNOW-BOUND.

2

Pedro II. of Brazil, 1825.

To Thee our full humanity,
  Its joys and pains, belong;
The wrong of man to man on Thee
  Inflicts a deeper wrong.

To do Thy will is more than praise,
  As words are less than deeds,

DECEMBER

And simple trust can find Thy ways
We miss with chart of creeds.

Alone, O Love ineffable!
Thy saving name is given;
To turn aside from Thee is hell,
To walk with Thee is heaven!
OUR MASTER.

3

Mary Lamb, 1764; Sir Frederick Leighton, 1830.

O LOVE Divine! — whose constant beam
Shines on the eyes that will not see,
And waits to bless us, while we dream
Thou leavest us because we turn from Thee!

All souls that struggle and aspire,
All hearts of prayer by Thee are lit;
And, dim or clear, thy tongues of fire
On dusky tribes and twilight centuries sit.

Nor bounds, nor clime, nor creed Thou know'st,
Wide as our need Thy favors fall;
The white wings of the Holy Ghost
Stoop, seen or unseen, o'er the heads of all.
THE SHADOW AND THE LIGHT.

DECEMBER

4

Thomas Carlyle, 1795.

FADE, pomp of dreadful imagery
  Wherewith mankind have deified
  Their hate, and selfishness, and pride!
Let the scared dreamer wake to see
  The Christ of Nazareth at his side!

The world sits at the feet of Christ,
  Unknowing, blind, and unconsoled;
  It yet shall touch His garment's fold,
And feel the heavenly Alchemist
  Transform its very dust to gold.
                  THE OVER-HEART.

5

Martin Van Buren, 1782; "E. Marlitt," 1825.

AGE brought him no despairing
Of the world's future faring;
In human nature still
He found more good than ill.

Hater of din and riot,
He lived in days unquiet;
And, lover of all beauty,
Trod the hard ways of duty.
                  AN AUTOGRAPH.

DECEMBER

6

R. H. Barham, 1788.

OTHERS shall sing the song,
Others shall right the wrong, —
Finish what I begin,
And all I fail of win.

What matter, I or they?
Mine or another's day,
So the right word be said
And life the sweeter made?

Hail to the coming singers!
Hail to the brave light-bringers!
Forward I reach and share
All that they sing and dare.
MY TRIUMPH.

7

Elizabeth Whittier, 1815.

As one who held herself a part
Of all she saw, and let her heart
　Against the household bosom lean,
Upon the motley-braided mat
Our youngest and our dearest sat,
Lifting her large, sweet, asking eyes,
　Now bathed in the unfading green
And holy peace of Paradise.

DECEMBER

I cannot feel that thou art far,
Since near at need the angels are;
And when the sunset gates unbar,
  Shall I not see thee waiting stand,
And, white against the evening star,
  The welcome of thy beckoning hand?
                              SNOW-BOUND.

8

Lady Anne Barnard, 1750.

NOR mine the hope of Indra's son,
  Of slumbering in oblivion's rest,
Life's myriads blending into one,
  In blank annihilation blest.

. . . .

No! I have friends in Spirit Land, —
Not shadows in a shadowy band,
  Not others, but themselves are they.
And still I think of them the same
As when the Master's summons came;
Their change, — the holy mornlight breaking
Upon the dream-worn sleeper, waking, —
  A change from twilight into day.
                              LUCY HOOPER.

9

John Milton, 1608.

THE new world honors him whose lofty plea
For England's freedom made her own more sure,

DECEMBER

Whose song, immortal as its theme, shall be
Their common freehold while both worlds endure.
                                    MILTON.
[*Inscription on the Memorial Window in St. Margaret's
Church, Westminster.*]

10

William Lloyd Garrison, 1805.

FROM lips that Sinai's trumpet blew
  We heard a tender undersong;
Thy very wrath from pity grew,
  From love of man thy hate of wrong.

Now past and present are as one;
  The life below is life above;
Thy mortal years have but begun
  The immortality of love.

Go, leave behind thee all that mars
  The work below of man for man;
With the white legions of the stars
  Do service such as angels can.
                                    GARRISON.

11

Hector Berlioz, 1803; Alfred de Musset, 1810.

O LIVING friends who love me!
O dear ones gone above me!
Careless of other fame,
I leave to you my name.

DECEMBER

Hide it from idle praises,
Save it from evil phrases:
Why, when dear lips that spake it
Are dumb, should strangers wake it?

Let the thick curtain fall;
I better know than all
How little I have gained,
How vast the unattained.
My Triumph.

12

John Jay, 1745; F. H. Hedge, 1805.

BEYOND the poet's sweet dream lives
　The eternal epic of the man.
He wisest is who only gives,
　True to himself, the best he can;
Who, drifting in the winds of praise,
　The inward monitor obeys;
And, with the boldness that confesses fear,
Takes in the crowded sail, and lets his conscience steer.
The Tent on the Beach.

13

Arthur Penrhyn Stanley, 1815; Phillips Brooks, 1835.

A TRUE life is at once interpreter and proof of the Gospel.
Introduction to Woolman's Journal.

DECEMBER

STILL shines the light of holy lives
Like star-beams over doubt;
Each sainted memory, Christlike, drives
Some dark possession out.
WILLIAM FORSTER.

14

Washington died, 1799.

OUR first and best! — his ashes lie
Beneath his own Virginian sky.
Forgive, forget, O true and just and brave,
The storm that swept above thy sacred grave!

For, ever in the awful strife
And dark hours of the nation's life,
Through the fierce tumult pierced his warning
    word,
Their father's voice his erring children heard!
THE VOW OF WASHINGTON.

15

La Rochefoucauld, 1613.

O LORD and Master of us all!
Whate'er our name or sign,
We own Thy sway, we hear Thy call,
We test our lives by Thine.

Our thoughts lie open to Thy sight;
And, naked to Thy glance,

DECEMBER

Our secret sins are in the light
Of Thy pure countenance.

Thy healing pains, a keen distress
 Thy tender light shines in;
Thy sweetness is the bitterness,
 Thy grace the pang of sin.
OUR MASTER.

16

George Whitefield, 1714; Jane Austen, 1775.

Lo! by the Merrimack Whitefield stands
In the temple that never was made by hands, —
Curtains of azure, and crystal wall,
And dome of the sunshine over all! —
A homeless pilgrim, with dubious name
Blown about on the winds of fame;
Now as an angel of blessing classed,
And now as a mad enthusiast.
Called in his youth to sound and gauge
The moral lapse of his race and age,
And, sharp as truth, the contrast draw
Of human frailty and perfect law;
Possessed by the one dread thought that lent
Its goad to his fiery temperament,
Up and down the world he went,
A John the Baptist crying, Repent!
THE PREACHER.

DECEMBER

17

Beethoven, 1770; John Greenleaf Whittier, 1807.

BESIDE that milestone where the level sun,
   Nigh unto setting, sheds his last, low rays
On word and work irrevocably done,
Life's blending threads of good and ill outspun,
   I hear, O friends! your words of cheer and praise,
Half doubtful if myself or otherwise.
   Like him who, in the old Arabian joke,
   A beggar slept and crownëd Caliph woke.
Thanks not the less. With not unglad surprise
I see my life-work through your partial eyes;
Assured, in giving to my home-taught songs
A higher value than of right belongs,
You do but read between the written lines
The finer grace of unfulfilled designs.
  1877.   RESPONSE.

18

Constitutional Amendment Abolishing Slavery, 1865.

How they pale,
Ancient myth and song and tale,
In this wonder of our days,
  When the cruel rod of war
  Blossoms white with righteous law,
And the wrath of man is praise!

    Ring and swing,
Bells of joy! On morning's wing

DECEMBER

Send the song of praise abroad!
With a sound of broken chains
Tell the nations that He reigns,
Who alone is Lord and God!
Laus Deo.

19

HE saw her lift her eyes; he felt
　The soft hand's light caressing,
And heard the tremble of her voice,
　As if a fault confessing.

"I'm sorry that I spelt the word:
　I hate to go above you,
Because," — the brown eyes lower fell, —
　"Because, you see, I love you!"

Still memory to a gray-haired man
　That sweet child-face is showing.
Dear girl! the grasses on her grave
　Have forty years been growing!

He lives to learn, in life's hard school,
　How few who pass above him
Lament their triumph and his loss,
　Like her, — because they love him.
In School-Days.

DECEMBER

20

LET the icy north-wind blow
The trumpets of the coming storm.
To arrowy sleet and blinding snow
You slanting lines of rain transform.
Young hearts shall hail the drifted cold,
As gayly as I did of old;
And I, who watch them through the frosty pane,
Unenvious, live in them my boyhood o'er again.
     THE LAST WALK IN AUTUMN.

21

Leopold von Ranke, 1795; Lord Beaconsfield, 1804.

DEAR to me these far, faint glimpses of the dual life of old,
Inward, grand with awe and reverence; outward, mean and coarse and cold;
Gleams of mystic beauty playing over dull and vulgar clay,
Golden-threaded fancies weaving in a web of hodden gray.

The great eventful Present hides the Past; but through the din
Of its loud life hints and echoes from the life behind steal in;

DECEMBER

And the lore of home and fireside, and the legendary rhyme,
Make the task of duty lighter which the true man owes his time.
                        THE GARRISON OF CAPE ANN.

22

Landing of the Pilgrims, 1620.

SAD Mayflower! watched by winter stars,
   And nursed by winter gales,
With petals of the sleeted spars,
   And leaves of frozen sails!

What had she in those dreary hours,
   Within her ice-rimmed bay,
In common with the wild-wood flowers,
   The first sweet smiles of May?
. . . .
"God wills it: here our rest shall be,
   Our years of wandering o'er;
For us the Mayflower of the sea
   Shall spread her sails no more."
. . . .
So live the fathers in their sons,
   Their sturdy faith be ours,
And ours the love that overruns
   Its rocky strength with flowers.
                        THE MAYFLOWERS.

DECEMBER

23

Sir Richard Arkwright, 1732; C. A. Sainte-Beuve, 1804.

ASK not why to these bleak hills
I cling, as clings the tufted moss,
To bear the winter's lingering chills,
The mocking spring's perpetual loss.
I dream of lands where summer smiles,
And soft winds blow from spicy isles,
But scarce would Ceylon's breath of flowers be sweet,
Could I not feel thy soil, New England, at my feet!
THE LAST WALK IN AUTUMN.

24

George Crabbe, 1754; Matthew Arnold, 1822.

WHO gives and hides the giving hand,
Nor counts on favor, fame, or praise,
Shall find his smallest gift outweighs
The burden of the sea and land.

Who gives to whom hath naught been given,
His gift in need, though small indeed
As is the grass-blade's wind-blown seed,
Is large as earth and rich as heaven.
GIVING AND TAKING.

DECEMBER

25

Christmas; Sir Isaac Newton, 1642; William Collins, 1720.

Our Friend, our Brother, and our Lord,
  What may Thy service be? —
Nor name, nor form, nor ritual word,
  But simply following Thee.

In vain shall waves of incense drift
  The vaulted nave around,
In vain the minster turret lift
  Its brazen weights of sound.

The heart must ring Thy Christmas bells,
  Thy inward altars raise;
Its faith and hope Thy canticles,
  And its obedience praise!

Our Master.

26

St. Stephen; Thomas Gray, 1716.

I listen, from no mortal tongue,
To hear the song the angels sung;
And wait within myself to know
The Christmas lilies bud and blow.

The outward symbols disappear
From him whose inward sight is clear;

DECEMBER

And small must be the choice of days
To him who fills them all with praise!
THE MYSTIC'S CHRISTMAS.

27

St. John Evangelist; Abigail Whittier (the Poet's Mother), died 1857.

AND *she* was with us, living o'er again
Her life in ours, despite of years and pain, —
The Autumn's brightness after latter rain.

Beautiful in her holy peace as one
Who stands, at evening, when the work is done,
Glorified in the setting of the sun!

Her memory makes our common landscape seem
Fairer than any of which painters dream,
Lights the brown hills and sings in every stream;

For she whose speech was always truth's pure gold
Heard, not unpleased, its simple legends told,
And loved with us the beautiful and old.
PROEM TO MABEL MARTIN.

28

Innocents' Day; C. M. Sedgwick, 1789.

OF such the kingdom! — Teach Thou us,
O Master most divine,
To feel the deep significance
Of these wise words of Thine!

DECEMBER

The haughty eye shall seek in vain
  What innocence beholds;
No cunning finds the key of heaven,
  No strength its gate unfolds.

Alone to guilelessness and love
  That gate shall open fall;
The mind of pride is nothingness,
  The childlike heart is all!
                              CHILD-SONGS.

29

W. E. Gladstone, 1809.

WHAT is really momentous and all-important with us is the present, by which the future is shaped and colored.
                              THE BETTER LAND.

THEN of what is to be, and of what is done,
  Why queriest thou? —
The past and the time to be are one,
  And both are now!
                              MY SOUL AND I.

30

GALLERY of sacred pictures manifold,
  A minster rich in holy effigies,
  And bearing on entablature and frieze
The hieroglyphic oracles of old.

DECEMBER

Along its transept aureoled martyrs sit;
And the low chancel side-lights half acquaint
The eye with shrines of prophet, bard, and saint,
Their age-dimmed tablets traced in doubtful writ!
But only when on form and word obscure
  Falls from above the white supernal light
  We read the mystic characters aright,
And life informs the silent portraiture,
Until we pause at last, awe-held, before
The One ineffable Face, love, wonder, and adore.
                                    THE BOOK.

31

James T. Fields, 1816.

HE knew each living pundit well,
  Could weigh the gifts of him or her,
And well the market value tell
  Of poet and philosopher.
But if he lost, the scenes behind,
Somewhat of reverence vague and blind,
Finding the actors human at the best,
No readier lips than his the good he saw confessed.

His boyhood fancies not outgrown,
  He loved himself the singer's art;
Tenderly, gently, by his own
  He knew and judged an author's heart.
No Rhadamanthine brow of doom
Bowed the dazed pedant from his room;

DECEMBER

And bards, whose name is legion, if denied,
Bore off alike intact their verses and their pride.
THE TENT ON THE BEACH.

BENEATH the moonlight and the snow
  Lies dead my latest year;
The winter winds are wailing low
  Its dirges in my ear.

I grieve not with the moaning wind
  As if a loss befell;
Before me, even as behind,
  God is, and all is well!
MY BIRTHDAY.

RICH gift of God! A year of time!
  What pomp of rise and shut of day,
What hues wherewith our Northern clime
  Makes autumn's dropping woodlands gay,
What airs outblown from ferny dells,
  And clover-bloom and sweet-briar smells,
What songs of brooks and birds, what fruits and flowers,
Green woods and moonlit snows, have in its round been ours!
THE LAST WALK IN AUTUMN.

www.ingramcontent.com/pod-product-compliance
Lightning Source LLC
Chambersburg PA
CBHW021304240426
43669CB00042B/1186